PLAY SOMETHING DANCY

The Tragic Tales of a Strip Club DJ

by

Dee Simon

Published by The Reach-Around Foundation

Author's Note: This book is a collection of short stories that occurred during a five-year period of my life. Regrettably, the events of this book are real; however, in order to protect myself from criminal prosecution and civil liability, names, locations, and identifying characteristics had to be changed. The dialogue and events have been recreated solely from memory, and I've smoked a lot of drugs since these events occurred. With that in mind, some of the dialogue and certain events may have been altered, combined, and even fabricated at times to convey the substance of what was said or what occurred.

Grateful acknowledgement is made for permission to reprint the following material: Excerpt from "Sweat Loaf" by the Butthole Surfers. Copyright © 1987 by Touch and Go Records. Used by permission. All rights reserved.

Cover design by Dee Simon & The Evil Twin (sashaloobkoff.com)
Cover photo: Dallas Stoeckel (dstokephoto.com)
Printed in the United States of America

ISBN-13: 978-0-9883474-6-5

for

Kessler

CONTENTS

Daddy, what does regret mean?

Well son, the funny thing about regret is,

It's better to regret something you have done,

Than to regret something you haven't done.

And by the way,

if you see your mom this weekend,

Be sure and tell her, Satan, Satan, Satan!

—Butthole Surfers

Lexi

"Are you going to fuck me?"

"What?"

"Are you going to fuck me?"

"What time is it?"

"I don't fucking know."

It felt like I had fractured my brain. My head throbbed intensely. I awoke to find a woman in her mid-to-late thirties with massive fake breasts straddling me. It was sometime in the early morning. Wincing in pain, I watched the sunlight slowly creep through the crumpled plastic blinds that covered the windows of my studio apartment. I had no recollection of how the woman ended up here. I just hoped that if I had fucked her I used a condom.

"Well, if you're not going to fuck me, do you have any more Jack?"

"Yeah, it's over there on the table."

She rolled off me and sauntered toward the kitchen table. Her skin was tanned and she had messy bleached-blonde hair. She grabbed a half-empty bottle of Jack Daniels and took a healthy swig. And then another. And then one more.

"Do you want some?"

"No."

Slowly the events from last night were drifting back into my mind. I remembered being at a punk show at Slims. Did the Dwarves play or was it Bottles and Skulls? Was it Thursday night or Friday night? I think it was Thursday night. I forget. When you work nights, the days seem to meld together. I must have run into this girl at the club. Things were beginning to make sense now. Her name was Lexi. That wasn't her real name. It was her stage name. I didn't bother to learn their real names. We worked together at the Ruby Club. I took a few seconds to admire her figure. She looked good for her age. I'm sure a healthy balance of cocaine and Pilates could make anyone look good. Lexi slammed the bottle down on the table and rifled through my kitchen drawers.

"What are you doing? What are you looking for?" I was clearly irritated.

"Where's the blow? I know we didn't do it all."

"I don't know. Fuck. You don't need it right now. You need to go back to bed."

I covered my head with a pillow and tried to ignore this annoyance in my personal space. Strippers are fun to have sex with, but it's definitely not fun trying to get them to leave the next morning. Lexi found my feeble attempt to hide rather amusing and ran over and jumped on top of me. Despite my protests, she pulled the blanket off and practically sliced through the skin with her sharp fingernails as she groped my crotch.

"Jesus. Would you leave me the fuck alone?"

"Damn. You're no fun, asshole. Do you have any porn?"

"Ugghh. Yeah. Somewhere. On top of the DVD player."

She hastily dismounted and threw the blanket over my head. I heard her flipping through my DVDs. I had a rather extensive collection of porn. Eventually, she came across one she fancied.

"How do you turn this thing on?"

10

"Give me that."

I snatched the remote out of her hand and started the movie. The face of a woman with an enormous cock in her mouth filled the screen. I tried to go back to sleep. Lexi lay back on the bed and played with herself. She was aroused within minutes and moaned loudly. It was obvious that she purposely put on quite a performance because she knew that I was trying to ignore her. She lay on top of me, lifted her back into an arch, and masturbated so fast that her hand was a blur. The moans transformed into screams and it was obvious to both of us that I wasn't going back to sleep. I had no choice but to fuck her. Maybe afterward she'll leave. My plan was to disappoint her on a grand scale. I would fuck her as quickly as possible and then go back to sleep. She started giving me head and I could tell she was well practiced. I think she might have done this one or two thousand times before. I slipped on a condom and turned her around so that I could enter her from behind. From this new perspective, I surveyed her vagina like a passerby who just happened upon a vehicular homicide. Without exaggeration, it looked like someone had ignited an M80 in a pastrami sandwich. Her labia were enormous and grey-blue in color. They literally hung in loose folds flanking her gaping hole. It was clear to me that I would be physically unable to please her. I've read that the average penis falls somewhere between five to seven inches. I would say that I'm well within that category; but Lexi definitely needed an above-average penis if she hoped to receive any pleasure from this sexual encounter. In fact, I think John Holmes would have shied away from this challenge. Regardless, I decided to give it my best shot. I plugged away for about five minutes when she began to moan softly. I assumed this was some type of act, but at least it was somewhat encouraging. Suddenly, she really got into it and

11

violently forced her ass against my thighs.

"Fuck me! You motherfucking piece of shit. Fuck my fucking pussyhole! Fuck me! Fuck me!" she screamed.

"Okay. I will. You got it. I'll fuck your pussyhole hard."

I tried to sound enthused. Well, as much as I could considering the situation. But I've never been good at sex talk. It's always been awkward for me. My friends tell me that you need to free yourself within the moment and say whatever comes to mind as long as it sounds sexy. But I've always felt too self-conscious hurling sexual epithets at a woman. It's unnatural and out of character for me. And if I start thinking too much about something appropriate to say, I lose focus on the matter at hand and then risk either prematurely ejaculating or, even worse, losing my erection. I'm like Woody Allen when it comes to sex. It's a complex psychological operation for me.

"Are you gonna fuck me with your hard cock? Are you? Fuck me now, you fucking shit bitch!"

Shit bitch? Really? I chose to ignore that one and began fucking her as hard and as fast as I could. But, despite my efforts, my penis was drowning in a sea of vagina. This wasn't a "hotdog in a hallway" situation; rather this was a "hotdog in a mineshaft" situation. Finally, I finished and fell forward in exhaustion. She didn't seem to realize that I was done and continued slamming her ass into me.

I pulled out and said plaintively, "Okay, okay, stop. It's over. I'm sorry if I didn't make you come."

"What? Is that it?"

"Yeah, that's it. That's all. I'm done."

"Fuck that. You're gonna eat me out, right?"

"No. Definitely not." A quick glance at her grey meat curtains reaffirmed my reluctance to stick my tongue anywhere near that. "Sorry. I'm going to have a smoke and go to back to bed. You're welcome to watch more porn." She stared at me in disbelief as I lit up a smoke and lay back on the bed. "I'm sorry. I feel like shit and need to sleep."

"Do you have a fucking vibrator?"

"No. Why would I have a vibrator?"

"I dunno. Lots of guys do." I watched her eyes dart around the room searching for something she could shove inside of her. God, I really wanted her to leave and let me go back to sleep. She jumped out of bed, bounded toward the kitchen, and after searching through several drawers, produced a claw hammer.

"This'll work," she said proudly and walked to the bed holding the hammer by the claw end so that the handle stuck straight up in the air. "Fuck me with this."

"What? That's a hammer."

"I know. And you're going to fuck me with it." She roughly shoved the tool into my hand, got down on all fours, and jutted her naked ass into the air.

With my cigarette dangling from my lips, I looked at her quizzically. "How exactly do you want me to fuck you with this?"

"Put a condom on it, stupid."

I was too stunned to be offended. I just sat there holding the hammer in my right hand and the cigarette in my left, watching her rhythmically sway her ass from side to side.

"Well, come on."

I grabbed a condom from the nightstand, rolled it over the wooden handle of the hammer, and apprehensively slid the tool inside of her. Lexi let out a loud gasp.

"Ohhh. Fuck me. Fuck me harder."

"Okay," I muttered while slowly sliding the hammer's handle in and out of her gaping pussy. Like any rational individual, I was hesitant to fuck her with it too hard lest I ruptured something. This was a construction tool, for fuck's sake.

"Would you fuck me with it? Fuck!" She violently shoved her ass back on the hammer's handle and almost knocked me over.

"I am fucking you with it."

"No, you're not."

She snatched the hammer from my hand, lay down on her back, and angrily shoved it between her spread thighs. With savage force, she jammed the tool inside of her again and again until she started screaming. "This is how you fuck me. This is how you fuck my pussy!"

With her mouth open and her eyes rolled upwards so that only the white parts were visible, she panted and screamed "fuck" over and over again while forcefully shoving the tool deep inside of her. It was like that scene from *The Exorcist*, except Linda Blair was masturbating with a crucifix, not a hammer. Her body thrashed about violently when she reached orgasm, and she started screaming out strings of profanities that I had never heard before, like "motherfuckerjesuscunt" and "dickshitasswhore." It sounded like she was swearing in tongues. Suddenly, the song "Baby Got Back" by Sir Mix-A-Lot started playing from somewhere in the room. Confused, I looked around trying to locate the source of the sound but to no avail. Lexi didn't seem to notice at all. The song stopped after about forty seconds or so and then I returned my attention to the writhing girl on my bed, watching her collapse and lie motionless with the hammer protruding from her swollen vagina. Speechless, I sat there with my cigarette—now a grey pillar of ash—resting between my lips.

"Are you all right?" I asked but received no response. For some reason, I thought it might be a good idea to retrieve the hammer, but before I could grab it she fiercely pushed my hand away.

"Don't touch me! Don't fucking touch me!"

"That's cool. I'm just glad you're conscious." I stumbled off the bed and went to the kitchen to fetch a glass of water for her. After that spectacle, it was the least I could do.

"What the fuck?"

"Pardon me?" I asked.

"What the fuck is this?" Lexi held the hammer in front of her and gazed perplexedly at the thick, dark red blood covering the handle.

"Holy shit! What the fuck is wrong with you?" A puddle of blood began to form between her legs, darkening the sheets. I ran to the bathroom, grabbed a towel off the floor, and rushed back to the bleeding woman. "Are you having your period or something?"

"No. I don't get those," she replied, stuffing the towel between her legs.

"Umm. Does it hurt? Are you in pain?"

"No. Not really. I know what it is. Fuck. I had an abortion on Tuesday."

"That was like two days ago. Aren't you supposed to take it easy for a week or two?"

"I know what I'm doing. This isn't the first time I had an abortion."

"Well, I don't know much about abortions, but I highly doubt it says in the abortion manual that it's acceptable to shove a fucking hammer in your pussy two days after you had the procedure. You probably tore open your uterus or something."

"Would you shut the fuck up? Give me a fucking cigarette." She held the towel between her legs. It was sodden with her dark red blood.

"You're losing a lot of blood. I think you need to go to the hospital." Once again, "Baby Got Back" began playing from somewhere. "What is that? Where's that coming from?"

"It's my phone."

"Oh." I've never been comfortable with obnoxious ringtones.

"Would you get my purse?" I looked under the bed and found her ridiculous pink ostrich-feather bag and handed it to her.

She pulled her phone out and flipped it open. "Fuck. It's Ron."

"Who's Ron?"

"My husband."

"Your husband? You're fucking married?"

"Calm down. We have an open relationship. He's an asshole anyway. I can't believe he called seven times. He knew I wasn't planning to come home last night. Asshole." She threw the phone on the floor and lifted the towel up a bit revealing the steady stream of blood still pouring out of her.

"I'm taking you to the hospital." I pulled on my jeans and threw on a shirt before scanning the room for Lexi's clothing. Her fishnet stockings and leather skirt lay in a pile at the foot of the bed. "Can you sit up? You need to get dressed." She moved to the side of the bed still holding the bloody towel, and I helped her slip on her top. She lifted up her legs as I gingerly pulled her skirt over her thighs.

16

"Here's your panties." I unintentionally handed them to her as if they belonged to a leper.

"Fuck. I'm sorry for my bloody pussy. Anyway, I don't think those are going to do much. You can keep 'em."

"Umm, thanks. Can you walk?"

"Yeah. I think so." I helped the wounded girl to her feet and she unsteadily shuffled toward the door holding the towel tightly between her legs. She leaned heavily on my left shoulder and I held her up like a fallen comrade as we carefully trudged down the dimly lit hallway toward the elevator. Both of us were tacitly aware of the awkwardness of this situation but chose not to acknowledge it as we marched onward in silence. It was a painfully sunny day in the San Francisco's Tenderloin neighborhood, and as my luck would have it, not a cab was in sight. I knew I should have called one. It's common knowledge that whenever you need a cab, they are nowhere to be found. I propped Lexi against the front gate of my building and stepped into the street waving my right hand in the air. After a few minutes, a yellow cab screeched to a stop in front of me, practically slamming into my kneecaps. I whipped open the back door, trying my best not to curse out the driver before walking over to fetch poor Lexi. She had lost a lot of blood and appeared pale and confused as I pushed her into the backseat of the cab, hoping that the driver hadn't already noticed the bloody towel between her legs.

"Take us to St. Mary's."

"Where do you need to go?" said the driver in English but with a thick Middle Eastern accent.

"We need to go to St. Mary's. Quickly please."

"What's the matter? Is she having baby?"

"The matter is none of your business. Just take us to St. Mary's."

"The girl is having a pregnancy?"

"No, she's fine."

"Then why you must go to hospital?"

"We just need to go there. Now. Fuck. Would you just shut the fuck up and drive us there?"

He shook his head, muttered something foreign, and sped down Ellis Street. We arrived at the hospital in less than six minutes. I threw him a wad of cash and pulled the bleeding girl out of the cab. She could hardly stand up and I practically had to carry her through the glass doors of the emergency room and up to the front desk. An overweight nurse looked at us with a jaded frown and asked for her insurance card.

"Do you have medical insurance?" I asked Lexi.

My question made her laugh out loud. "Yeah. It's right next to my Platinum Visa."

I begged the nurse, "Please, this is an emergency. She's bleeding heavily. Can we just see a doctor and sort this out later?"

The nurse let out a heavy sigh and handed me the registration forms. Another equally overweight nurse ambled over pushing a wheelchair and helped Lexi sit down. She threw her purse at me just before the nurse wheeled her down a hallway through a curtain and out of sight.

"Should I go with her?"

"Just sit down and fill out the forms," the nurse said with her trademark sigh.

There were hardly any open seats in the waiting room. I sat in the first seat I could find next to a homeless man with a severe eye infection. He was shaking his head from side to side, muttering, "fuck this shit" over and over again. I ignored him and concentrated on the forms the

18

nurse gave me. It took several minutes before I realized that there was no way I could properly fill these out. I didn't even know Lexi's real first name, let alone her surname or social security number. I leaned back in the chair, holding her pink ostrich-feather purse and the hospital registration forms in my lap and wishing that I could travel back in time to last night at the bar. As soon as Lexi had approached me, I would have pretended not to recognize her, left the bar alone, and at this very moment, I would have been sleeping in my warm bed rather than sitting in a hospital waiting room next to a diseased homeless person. Her phone rang again, playing her obnoxious "Baby Got Back" ringtone. This caught the attention of my neighbor, and he laughed and sang along in a gravelly voice, "*Girl got an Oakland booty. Bitch got back.* Yeah. I love that shit." He motioned for me to bump fists with him, but I shook my head "no" and stood up from the chair, pretending that I had some pressing matter that needed my attention. It's my personal policy not to touch the homeless. He frowned and hissed, "Nice purse, faggot," and erupted into spasms of wheezy laughter. This prompted the group of homeless people sitting across from us to start laughing as well. I had reached my threshold. I contemplated leaving Lexi's purse at the front desk with the fat nurse and then heading home. But then my conscience grew heavy as I realized that I was partly at fault for this state of affairs and I went outside to have a cigarette. Lexi's phone rang again. I felt I should answer it because obviously her husband was concerned about the welfare of his wayward wife. Someone had to tell him that she was at the emergency room. If he called again, I resolved to answer it. Five minutes later, "Baby Got Back" rang out and this time I answered. "Hello."

"Who the fuck is this?"

"This is Dave. I'm answering Lexi's phone."

"Lexi? Where the fuck is Amber?"

Amber must be Lexi's real name. "Umm, Amber's at the hospital right now."

"What? The hospital? Who the fuck are you? Why do you have her goddamn phone?"

"I'm one of Amber's friends and I'm at the hospital with her. I'm holding her purse for her, and I answered her phone because it kept ringing."

"Fuck yeah, it kept ringing. I been calling it all morning. What? Were you fucking her last night?'

"Well, she spent the night at my house and injured herself this morning, so now we're at St. Mary's Hospital."

"You didn't answer my question. Were you fucking my wife last night?"

"Listen. I don't think you should be concerned with that right now. I think you should be concerned with your wife being in the emergency room."

"Listen, fuckstick. Don't tell me what I should be concerned with. I'll be concerned with whatever the fuck I want to be concerned with. Were you fucking her last night?"

I couldn't believe I was having a conversation like this. I should be in my bed right now.

"Yes. I fucked your wife last night. Is that what you want to hear?"

"Who's this again? Rick? Juan?"

"This is Dave. I work with your wife."

"The DJ?"

"Yeah."

"I heard about you. She talks about you all the time. DJ Dirty Sanchez, her favorite fucking DJ. "

"Listen. Your wife's in the hospital. I think you should come see her."

"I knew she was fucking somebody last night. I could feel it. Fucking whore. They're all fucking whores."

"Dude, your wife's in the hospital. You should come see her."

"All right. Where you at again?'

"St. Mary's on Hyde and Bush."

"All right. I'm coming. Fuckin' A. I don't need this shit." Click.

I went back into the waiting room to wait for Lexi's husband. It was noon already and I was beyond exhausted. My shift started at six and I was dreading the thought of having to work all night after dealing with this. The only open seat was next to the same homeless man with the eye infection. I collapsed into the chair and noticed him staring at me warily with his one good eye. I think he was still upset because I hadn't bumped his calloused fist. Lexi's husband Ron showed up about an hour and a half later. I knew who he was because he had been calling her phone for the past half hour telling me that he would be there soon with the girls. I observed Ron standing in the middle of the waiting room anxiously punching numbers into his cellphone, trying to determine how I'd approach him, when "Baby Got Back" started playing and his head jerked over to where I was sitting. He immediately walked towards me with his daughters closely in tow. The girls were quite young. The oldest looked about ten and the youngest about six. All three had long, yellow-blonde hair like their mother. Ron had to be at least forty years old. He was a stocky man about 5'9", maybe 180 pounds. He was much larger than me. His hair was pulled back into a greasy ponytail, and he was wearing a black faded Miller High Life T-shirt and tight blue jeans and mirrored aviator shades. He took off his sunglasses and stood there staring at me for a few seconds before putting them back on. Honestly, I wasn't quite certain whether he was going to embrace me or punch me in the face. I hoped for the former. I stood up to greet him and hesitantly extended my hand. He studied it for a second or two, shook twice, and then angrily released it. His irritation was palpable. In fact, he didn't even bother to introduce himself. The awkward silence was soon broken by the shrill voice of his youngest daughter who couldn't have been older than six or seven.

"Daddy, who's this guy?"

Ron turned to her and said, "He's the guy your mother fucked last night."

As soon as he said this, all three girls focused their undivided attention on me. The youngest girl then inquired, "You fucked my mommy?"

I didn't know how to respond to this. "I'm not going to answer that. I don't think it's appropriate to talk about that in front of children. Your wife's in one of the rooms right now. You should probably talk to a nurse or something." I handed Ron the registration forms and Lexi's purse. Ron was still glaring at me. He refused to take the purse or the forms from me.

"Don't you fucking tell me how to raise my kids. You can fuck my wife, but don't you ever tell me how to raise my fucking kids."

I really needed to defuse this situation. "Listen. I didn't mean to tell you how to raise your kids, okay? You can raise them any way you want.

It's none of my business. I'm sorry for that. I just didn't want to talk about that in front of them"

"You're damn right you're sorry. You're a sorry sack of shit. I don't fucking care what you say to them. Besides, that one isn't even mine." He said this while pointing at the youngest girl with the shrill voice. Ron snatched the purse and the forms out of my hand and stormed off towards the nurse's desk, leaving me with his three daughters. I watched him having a heated discussion with the overweight nurse at the desk. He scribbled something on the forms, tossed them at the woman, and stomped back towards us. "She's going to be in there a couple more hours. We can't go in yet." Ron's cellphone was vibrating and he agitatedly glanced at it before shoving it back in his pocket. "How long you been here?"

"I've been here for almost two hours and I really need to get home. So, since this is all taken care of, it was good to meet you and your daughters. Tell Lexi, I mean Amber, that I'll see her at work and to take care of herself. I hope everything works out."

"Hold on a second, tough guy." His phone was vibrating again and this time he answered it. "What the fuck do you want? I'm busy. I'm with my fucking kids. No, I can't come over right now. Can you wait a couple hours?" He hung up the phone and looked at me entreatingly. "Hey, man, can you do me a huge favor? I need you to watch the girls for a minute."

"Dude, I really can't do that. I have to go work. I'm sorry but I can't."

"Come on, man. I let you fuck my wife and I don't beat your fucking ass. The least you can do is watch my kids for a fucking half hour while I go pick up some money. I'll be right back. They're good girls."

I anxiously glanced over at the girls. The oldest twirled her hair around her forefinger and made kissing gestures at me. "Listen, I really can't do this. I have to go to work."

"Come on, man. Do this one thing for me. It's the least you can do. I really need to get this money. It will be a half hour tops."

I felt genuine sympathy for the guy and reluctantly acquiesced. After all, I did fuck his wife last night and now she's in the emergency room. "All right. Half an hour. And then I have to leave. Seriously."

"Thanks, buddy." He crouched down and grabbed all the girls together. "Listen, honeys. I need you to stay with Dirty Sanchez over here. Daddy's gonna be right back." With that, he patted his eldest daughter on her head, stood up, flashed me the thumbs up sign, and then briskly walked away.

The girls stood there staring at me as if they were waiting for some type of direction. I'm not good with children. And they could sense my discomfort. Children have this uncanny ability to sense when they're not wanted and then take full advantage of the situation. I looked around the waiting room, trying to find some place where we could all sit down. I motioned them towards four open seats in the corner of the room. I had no idea what preteens do in their spare time. I scanned the room for coloring books or *Highlights* magazines to give them. There was a stack of old *People* magazines on a table next to my seat and I handed them to the children. "Here you go. You can read, right? Your dad will be back in a minute." This day had become a veritable nightmare. The girls apathetically flipped through the magazines and whispered amongst themselves. I heard the youngest one giggling but tried my best to ignore them all while flipping through a *Reader's Digest*. I stopped at an article about a camper who survived a grizzly bear attack and pretended to read it. I don't think anyone under the age of sixty is allowed to read *Reader's Digest*. Out of the corner of my eye, I noticed the youngest daughter, her knees balanced on the arm of her chair, staring at me with the same wide-eyed fascination that she would have for a burn victim attempting to apply lip gloss. I focused my complete attention on the miniature magazine in my hands and purposely avoided all eye contact. Perhaps if I acted like she didn't exist, she'd leave me alone. Of course, I was wrong. She tapped my shoulder with her little finger and continued tapping for about twenty seconds until I had no choice but to address her.

"What do you want?"

"Did you really have sex with my mommy?" she asked in her sickeningly adorable "Cindy Lou Who" voice.

"I don't want to talk about this with you."

"Why not?"

"Because you're like six years old and should not be concerned with grown-up things." As soon as I said this, all three started to giggle.

The oldest daughter, who had been making the kissing gestures earlier, then said flippantly, "My mom has sex with lots of men, so don't think you're special."

"I don't think I'm special. I don't think I'm anything. This conversation's over."

"Is Dirty Sanchez your real name?"

"No. It's my DJ name, unfortunately."

"What's your real name?"

"My real name's Dave."

"That's a boring name."

"Fair enough. What's your name?"

"I'm Tessa." Pointing to her sisters, she said, "This is Angelynne. And this is Becca."

I could tell by their names that they would most likely follow their mother's career path.

"It's nice to meet all of you. Now sit there and read your magazines. Your dad should be back soon."

The youngest girl, Becca, dropped her magazine and looked up at me. "I'm hungry. Do you have McDonalds?"

"No. I don't."

"Can you get some?"

I flashed her an exasperated look. "There's no McDonalds here. This is a hospital."

"I'm hungry. We haven't eaten all day." All the girls were now looking at me like despondent golden retriever puppies abandoned at the side of a lonely country road.

"Uggh, I'm sure there's a vending machine around here." At this point, I could understand the reason Lexi had her recent abortion. "Come on. Let's go find some food." We walked towards the main nurses' desk where I asked about the cafeteria. The nurse pointed to a hallway to our left and we went off in search of food. Surprisingly, the cafeteria offered a variety of food options. The girls specifically requested ice cream sundaes and luckily the cafeteria had them. I bought three sundaes and we sat down at one of the green formica tables. While I watched them eat, I resolved to get a vasectomy at this very same hospital next week.

Becca, with vanilla ice cream dripping from her chin, turned to me and asked, "Do you love my mommy?"

"No. Not exactly. I'm friends with your mommy."

"My daddy doesn't love my mommy either. He calls her a dirty cocksucking whore." When she said this, her sisters laughed hysterically.

"You shouldn't say things like that."

"Why not?"

"Because you're a little girl, and little girls don't talk about things like that. Jesus. I need a cigarette, so let's finish our ice cream and go outside." Before they finished, I took off towards the exit. They followed behind me. Ron had been gone for well over an hour. I was past the point of compassion and was currently figuring out ways I could abandon them here without anyone noticing. I even contemplated slipping the homeless guy with the eye infection a twenty and asking him to watch them. Before we reached the revolving glass doors, Ron entered with his arm wrapped around the shoulders of a blonde girl in her early twenties.

"Hey there, buddy. How's the babysitting going?" Both he and his lady friend chuckled at this.

Now I was angry. "Look, man, you have some wonderful children. I have to go. I hope your wife's all right."

Ron released his girlfriend and turned to face me. He suddenly threw his arms out and clutched me in a tight embrace that lasted for about fifteen awkward seconds. "Thanks, man. I really had to get my swerve on, if you know what I mean," he said, patting my back.

I broke free of his embrace. "No, I don't know what you mean. You're an asshole, and I have to go now."

"Come on, man. I'm the asshole? Who were you banging last night? Oh yeah, my fucking wife. Listen, man, this open marriage shit is bullshit. Someone always gets hurt. No fucking way around it. But I can play that game too." He looked over at the twenty-something girl playing with his eldest daughter's blonde hair and slapped her playfully on the ass. "It's just so much easier for a bitch to find some dick. You know what I'm sayin'? They can go to any bar and get laid. Fuck, they can get laid on the bus. Fucking whores. They're all fucking whores." His eyes were bloodshot and his breath reeked of whiskey.

Becca looked up at Ron and then at me and asked, "Daddy, is Mommy really a whore?"

Ron turned towards the girl, bent down, and held her tiny face between his hands. "Yes she is, baby, your mom's a dirty whore, but I love her and she's gonna be okay."

And this was my exit. Without saying goodbye, I turned around and practically ran out of the hospital. I'd be lying if I said I didn't feel sorry for those children, but they weren't my concern. My concern was that it was after 5:00 PM and my shift started in less than an hour.

You Can't Make a Ho a Housewife

I rarely told anyone that I was a strip club DJ. When someone asked what I did for a living, I'd say I worked in radio. Not that being a strip club DJ is any less embarrassing than being a wedding DJ or roller rink DJ; I just didn't want to deal with the "do you get to fuck all the strippers every night" question or, even worse, the derisive impersonations: "Give it up for Stacey swinging on the pole tonight. Yeah, Stacey." I just didn't want to go there, so I'd lie and say I worked in radio. Well, it wasn't an outright lie. I really wanted to work in radio but just couldn't land a commercial gig. I had wanted to work in radio since my thirteenth birthday when I saw Oliver Stone's film *Talk Radio*. While my friends were briefly entertained by the strong language but ultimately bored, I was utterly enthralled with Barry Champlain, the shock jock played by Eric Bogosian. Two years later I heard Howard Stern for the first time and I had found my calling. I got a college degree in broadcasting and landed a few gigs in Detroit and the Chicago suburbs before relocating to San Francisco in the late nineties with the goal of becoming a famous radio talk show host.

I soon discovered that it's not all that simple to waltz into the number five radio market in the country and land an afternoon-drive shift. In fact, I learned that it's nearly impossible unless you're a hot chick with a massive rack. I mailed countless demos but with little success. There were no call backs, only rejection letters stating that my

29

credentials were "indeed" impressive but the position had been filled. I managed to find an unpaid gig at KUSF 90.3 FM, a local, non-commercial radio station, as the host of a late-night metal radio show called Rampage Radio. The show was recorded live every Sunday night from 2:00 to 8:00 AM and was one of the longest-running metal radio programs in the country. In the beginning, I was really inspired and believed that this was my ticket to broadcasting stardom. I interviewed local metal and punk bands and became the unwavering voice of the underground music scene. But after several years, the show devolved into a six-hour methamphetamine-fueled after party featuring a cast of rock-and-roll casualties, goth scenesters, homeless punks, and tranny street hookers. After one regrettable night involving several rails of speed, a six-pack of chocolate pudding, and a stripper named Dallas, I earned the moniker "Dirty Sanchez," which took me three years and several job changes to finally shake. Looking back, that unfortunate nickname and a nasty methamphetamine habit were the only things I ever got from that show.

Soon, I found myself broke and living in one of the most expensive cities in the country. It was then that I came to the bitter realization that I was going to have to put my radio dreams on hiatus and find real employment. It was the start of the new millennium, and San Francisco was experiencing the dotcom explosion. Thousands of people from around the country moved to the Bay Area in search of a quick fortune with some Internet start-up company. Employment was abundant, and I easily landed a production job at *The Industry Standard*, a weekly newsmagazine about the dotcom industry. The magazine was wildly successful, making millions from the booming economy, and like most people working for an Internet start-up, I was paid an exorbitant amount of money to do very little. Life was good, until it all came crashing down. And it crashed hard. In early 2001, the economy took a nosedive, and practically overnight, the ubiquitous Internet start-ups fell like overpriced, valueless dominoes. In a few short months, *The Industry Standard* had no choice but to shutter its doors. They were so broke that they couldn't even give their last remaining employees a severance package. I recall leaving the building with a box of red sharpies and three packets of Post-It notes. Once more, I found myself unemployed in San Francisco, but this time everyone in the city was unemployed.

I still hadn't discarded my dream to work in radio, and every day I would send out demo packages to unresponsive radio stations throughout California, Oregon, and Washington. My daily routine involved waking around 1:00 PM, masturbating to Internet porn, scouring the various job websites looking for a promising opportunity, and then off to FedEx to send out some demos. One day, when I was returning home from FedEx, I bumped into Hollywood, my old weed dealer and frequent guest on Rampage Radio. He was hard to miss being a 6'5" white guy with blonde dreads and a white polyester leisure suit. Hollywood worked at Teasers, a strip club located on San Francisco's infamous Broadway strip. He mentioned that with my radio experience, he could probably get me an audition at one of the smaller clubs on the strip. I was interested in anything that would give me a paycheck, and he said he'd check back with me in a few days. Two days later, Hollywood called and told me that the Doll House, a small nudie bar, had just fired one of their DJs, and he had set me up with an audition with Casey, the daytime manager. Up until that fateful day, I had never fancied myself a strip club DJ. Honestly, I've never really been a "strip club guy." Sure, I've been to a few strip clubs over the years, but those weren't places that I frequented on a regular basis. I usually went to a strip club for special occasions, such as a bachelor party or a friend's birthday. I was instantly reminded of that *Kids in the Hall* skit with the Chicken Lady at the strip club. A mulleted and mustachioed Bruce McCullough was the emcee, and he used lines like, "One hand clapping against the other makes a very nice sound for Rooster Boy." For some reason, the thought of myself wearing a sequined blazer with a red bowtie and asking people to give it up for Candy, was strangely appealing. I told Hollywood that I was very interested and thanked him profusely.

The audition was the next day around noon. It surprised me how nervous I was for it. I had more butterflies in my stomach walking into that sleazy nudie bar than when I interviewed for my 70K salaried position at the dotcom magazine. This was my first live audition. I had been doing radio for a few years, but as any performer would attest, addressing a live audience is far more gut-wrenching than talking into a microphone in a studio. I was expected to entertain people. They depended on me to give them a show worth their entrance fee. Not to mention, I also had to deal with strippers. I nervously ambled towards the club, strongly considering abandoning this ridiculous venture altogether, when a hairy, muscular arm grabbed my shoulder and pulled me towards the dark entrance of the Doll House. The arm was attached to a husky Latin American fellow who whispered in my ear that he was going to hook me up with the lady of my dreams. His breath was a mélange of marijuana, pizza, and malt liquor.

"Black girls, white girls, Asians, lovely Latinas. Whatever you want. We got 'em. Just ten to get in, but for you, I'm going to make it five. How 'bout it?" He kept nodding his shaved head in affirmation, smiling widely, and tightly clenching my shoulders, pulling me closer to the entrance.

"Thanks, but I'm here to audition for the DJ position."

He instantly released me, stuck his head through the purple velvet curtain behind the cash register, and screamed, "Case, DJ's here." Then he turned away and began a conversation with a lithe, scantily clad blonde girl who was leaning against a mirrored wall, smoking a cigarette. I stood there hovering at the entrance of the club, unsure if I should just walk in or wait until Casey came to fetch me. From the outside, one was not privy to the goings-on inside the club. I could hear Prince's "Get Off" blasting from inside, but I could not see if anyone was dancing to it because of the long, purple curtain separating the interior of the club from the entryway. For a minute or two, I studied the many cigarette burns and miscellaneous stains in the curtain, when Casey poked his head through the opening and beckoned me inside. I followed him inside the club and entered a dimly lit room slightly larger than a middle-school classroom. There was a stage in the center illuminated by flashing red, blue, yellow, and green lights. A fully nude girl, barely eighteen, gyrated on her hands and knees on the side of the stage directly in front of the only customer in the place. He was staring intensely at her spread pussy as if bewitched by some Santerian pussy trance. A folded dollar bill hung loosely from his lips. It was really dark, and it took a few moments for my eyes to adjust. The only source of light other than the stage lights was a mirror ball that cast little white circles that danced playfully across the walls of the room. What stood out most clearly in my mind and took me the longest to grow accustomed to was the horrendous stench that permeated the place. It was like someone mixed perfume, Lysol, semen, sweat, cigarettes, and vomit in a bucket and splashed the vile mixture all over the room. It actually made me retch.

"Pleased to meet you, Dirty Sanchez, and welcome to the Doll House," Casey said, extending his hand.

I shook his hand and replied, "You can call me Dave. Hollywood knows me as Dirty Sanchez from my radio show, but my real name's Dave. Thanks for setting this up. This is my first time here."

"Really? It's a wonderful place filled with mystery and intrigue. Like Fantasy Island with sluts. You'll grow to love it here. Let me show you the booth."

I followed him to a small DJ booth situated in the back of the club. It consisted of an old amplifier, a receiver, two heavily used CD players, and a microphone, all hidden behind a six-foot, mirror-covered wall. To the right of the stereo equipment was a book of CDs and an erasable board with four names scrawled on it. The DJ on duty was a tall, young black man who appeared less than pleased at having to be working that afternoon.

"Terrell, this is Dirty Sanchez. He's going to audition for your job," Casey said sarcastically.

"My name's Dave. Nice to meet you."

Terrell shook my hand and grinned. "Dirty Sanchez? I don't even want to know where that came from."

"It's my radio name. I didn't pick it. Long story."

"You're auditioning? Good. That means I don't have to do this shit no more."

Terrell was actually a manager but was covering the shift since they had just fired the regular daytime DJ. The booth was barely large enough to fit two people, so I stood to his right and listened intently while he explained how to operate the equipment. He started showing me how to

34

adjust the volume on the microphone when he noticed that the Prince song was coming to an end. Abruptly, his attention shifted away from me and all at once he assumed the character of a strip club DJ. Gripping the microphone in his left hand and rewinding the track on the CD with his right, he said, "Gentlemen, let's make a little noise for Jasmine. She's ready to give you a private show in the Doll House VIP Room. Take advantage while you still can." His voice possessed this inflection of tawdriness that was not present in our conversation beforehand. He slowly faded out the Prince song and faded in an R&B song that I didn't recognize. A new girl wearing a pink thong and bikini top now approached the stage. "Okay, I want everyone to clap their hands for this next hottie. We got Chastity center stage." He didn't seem to care that there was only one customer in the room, and he wasn't clapping at all. Terrell shut off the microphone and resumed the tutoring session; the cheesy strip club DJ intonation had completely vanished. He wanted me to listen to him put a few girls onstage and then try it out for myself. The nervousness did not subside. After listening for about ten minutes, Terrell felt that I was ready to announce the next girl, and shifted positions with me. I was now behind the microphone, butterflies swarming in my stomach. Trite, trashy phrases swarmed through my mind while I attempted to figure out what I was about to say. In hindsight, I don't know why I was so bothered. The audience consisted of an old pervert, Casey, Terrell, and three bored strippers. Yet, there I was scared shitless. Twenty seconds left of the current girl's song. This was it. I placed my lips near the microphone and uttered the first of many cheesy lines in my strip club DJ career:

35

"All right, fellas, let's get those hands clapping out there for Chastity. That sexy lady is stepping off the stage and onto your lap for a wet and wild ride. Get yourself a private show before you go."

The words formed freely without hesitation. I introduced the next girl and mixed in a new song. It was simple. There was no reason to be nervous. From their satisfied expressions, I could tell that Casey and Terrell were impressed. They had me work the mic for the better part of an hour till Casey told me that he thought I sounded great and would be perfect for the job. Terrell got back on the mic, and I followed Casey to the back office to fill out paperwork. We headed down a dark hallway lit only by pink neon lights and passed by a row of lap-dance booths. The booths were the size of a walk-in closet with a black velour curtain in lieu of a door, and a bench covered in cheap pink vinyl. There were about eight booths in total, some of which had exotic themes, like the Italian room or the African Safari room. Other than a chipped and faded mural of the Leaning Tower of Pisa, I struggled to comprehend how this dark closet that smelled like bleach, semen, and cotton candy perfume reminded anyone of Italy. The office was located at the end of the hallway, adjacent to the last booth that seemed to have a pirate theme. Casey ushered me in and swiftly shut and locked the door. The office was barely larger than the lap-dance booths and barren except for two folding chairs, a desk covered in paper and fast-food wrappers, and a couple boxes containing porn videos, dildos, and Doll House T-shirts. The walls were plastered with the dancers' schedules and promotional posters of upcoming feature entertainers. Casey sat down at the desk, threw some papers to the floor, and emptied the powdery contents of a small baggie onto the newly cleared area.

36

"Do you mind if I smoke?" Casey asked while torching a cigarette.
"Not at all. Can I bum one?"

He handed me a cigarette and a book of matches. "You want some Evel Knieval?" As we became better friends, I learned that Casey invariably used a euphemism for methamphetamine, which allowed him to make light of his addiction.

Though I was a bit surprised that he was so cavalier about snorting lines of meth with a complete stranger, at the same time I felt this was some type of bonding ritual. "Yeah, for sure."

I noticed that he was cutting up lines with his right hand and stroking the scar on his face with his left. To the uninitiated, Casey had a rather daunting visage. I'll never forget that face. He stood about six feet and was surprisingly well built for an addict. With broad shoulders and a thick neck, one could tell that he was a probably a wrestler or football player in high school. He had a serious case of adult acne, but his most distinguishable feature was a sickle-shaped scar that ran from the corner of his left eye to the side of his mouth. He wore his hair pulled back in a tight ponytail and always had on dark black sunglasses even indoors and at night. Casey would say that his eyes were sensitive to fluorescent light, but the truth was that he was incredibly self-conscious of the color of his eyes. His left eye was light blue, and his right eye was dark brown. He once told me that this was a rare condition called heterochromia, which he had had since he was a child. It was rare to see him without his shades.

Casey appreciated the scar on his face because it distracted people from his eye discoloration. Every shift, he'd be asked by at least three dancers about the origin of his scar, and every time he'd create a new ghastly tale about what happened. From Chinese gangsters slicing his face open over a sex-slave deal gone awry, to his face being ripped apart by a dancer's stiletto while she was high on PCP, I would hear some of the most outlandish stories about the scar on that man's face. He felt justified in lying about it due to the inquisitor's lack of tact. And the gullible dancers believed his stories despite the absurdity and would relay the story to their coworkers and eventually to me. By then, the tall tale had been so twisted and distorted that Casey himself would deny even telling it in the first place. When I worked with him, we would head to his apartment after our shift to smoke drugs, drink beer, and discuss the rumors we had heard about his scar that day. One night, we sat in his apartment smoking some weed, and he revealed the true origin of his scar to me. He had actually received it while managing at Temptations, a seedy club located downtown. A rather disheveled customer had come into the club that night and began harassing some of the dancers. Casey assumed he was a harmless crackhead who probably lived in the neighborhood, and asked him politely to settle down or he'd have to leave. The man calmed down for about ten minutes and then resumed his previous ranting, except this time he directed all his aggression towards one particular dancer named Rosa. Rosa was a fiery Latina with a short fuse and a propensity for violence. She often proclaimed to be the girlfriend of a cartel member and would threaten management if they dared to cross her. He couldn't recall what the crackhead had said to her, but nevertheless, it pissed her off, and she jumped off the stage topless and began spitting, swearing, and scratching at the man's face. Casey and one of the bouncers immediately separated them, and the bouncer hauled the man outside of the building where he and a colleague proceeded to beat the living hell out of the guy. Several nights later, Casey was outside smoking a cigarette with one of the bouncers, and the same crackhead returned to the club. Casey calmly told him that he was permanently barred and needed to head elsewhere. The man stood there glaring at him and without warning smashed a 40-ounce bottle of Steel Reserve across his face. With his face split open, he wrestled the man to the ground and held him in a headlock until police arrived. He then slipped into unconsciousness and woke up in an emergency room high on Demerol with little feeling on the right side of his face. After seven hours of reconstructive surgery, he left the hospital with a heavily stitched sickle-shaped wound initiating under his left eye and curving down to the corner of his mouth. In time, he actually grew to appreciate the scar, because not only was it an interesting and frequent topic of conversation, it also seemed to attract his preferred type of woman. His only regret was that he would have felt better had he been hit with a bottle of Jack Daniels. "At least, I drink Jack," he'd glibly remark.

"Here. This one's yours," Casey said as he handed me a small straw.

I snorted the massive line, and it burned my nasal passage like powdered napalm. "Fuck. That hurts. Who'd you get that from? Hitler?" I muttered, wincing in pain.

"Calm down. It's not that bad. I've done three already."

"Jesus. I'll do half next time. I'm not a professional."

"So, you come highly recommended from my boy, Hollywood. And you sounded fine out there, but that's not saying much. You could sound like the dude from *Sling Blade* and the perverts wouldn't notice. All they care about is the pussy in their face."

"Yeah, I could tell. It was like they were in a trance."

"That's how it always is. Especially with the Mexicans. They have this mutant ability to stare at a girl's pussy for six hours straight without blinking. It's uncanny. So, you're totally hired. Can you start tomorrow?"

"Yeah, thanks. What time should I be here?"

"You'll be working day shifts Monday through Friday from noon till about seven. The night shift starts around seven, but the DJs are always late. There's no sense of time around here." Casey shuffled through the stack of papers on the desk. He found what he was looking for and handed me a manila envelope filled with paperwork. "I'll need you to fill these out by tomorrow."

"All right."

"Stop. Do you hear that?"

"Hear what? 'Bizarre Love Triangle'?" The New Order song had been playing for the past two minutes.

"That. Listen," Casey said with his index finger pointing in the air.

"I don't hear anything except for the end of the New Order song."

"No. Listen. The girl in the booth next to us is sucking a dick right now."

"No way. How do you know?"

"I have a finely tuned ear for illicit cocksucking during a lap dance. It's a vital managerial skill."

"You're tripping. I don't hear that at all."

"That's because you're not a manager. Care to wager $20?"

"You want to bet $20 that the girl in the booth next door is sucking a dick right now?"

"Exactly."

"All right. I'll bet." We shook hands, and Casey leaned forward and finished the last line on the desk.

Staring up at the ceiling, he said, "You're right. This stuff is shit. It fucking burns. Now I want my $20."

We walked out of the office and stood in front of the velvet curtain door of the pirate-themed lap-dance booth. I could hear shuffling noises and muffled movements but nothing that sounded like a blow job. Casey stood there with his index finger in the air and mouthed the words "listen." I still couldn't hear anything. Without warning, he threw back the curtain to reveal a stark naked dancer standing above a crouching man who looked Mexican. She was straddling his face with his mouth buried between her legs. He was naked from the waist down and furiously stroking his penis. Once the curtain flew open, the dancer shrieked and immediately jumped off of him.

"I wasn't doin' nothin'. Just dancing. Nothin'. Seriously," she pleaded.

Casey, pointed at the girl and said, "You're fired. Get your things and leave. Now." He moved his finger in the direction of the crouching customer. "You. Put your pants back on and get the fuck out of here." He then turned towards me and said, "And you owe me $20."

"Well, technically, she wasn't sucking his dick. He was eating her out. So, I think you owe me $20."

"Fuck you. Bet's off."

The dancer picked up her outfit and ashamedly slipped by us, muttering to herself that she "wasn't doin' nothing" and that this was "some bullshit." The customer fumbled for his pants while yelling, "Yo, you can't make a ho a housewife. You can't. It don't work like that. You can't."

"Would you just get the fuck out of here? Goddamn. Fucking perverts," Casey said with disgust.

41

The guy shuffled past us, buttoning his trousers, still declaring the contrast between hos and housewives. To this day, I still don't understand the meaning of his statement. So, it was methamphetamine and illegal blowjobs that marked my entrance into the perverse, sordid, and financially rewarding lifestyle that I led for the next five years. Sometimes I wonder if I had hastily exited that establishment and found a job at a place like Kinkos, would it have saved my relationship with my ex-fiancé or kept me from a drug addiction that took several years to get rid of? Honestly, I doubt it.

Frustration McLonelys

Human existence is motivated by sex. Blame it on the media, if that's what justifies your misdeeds. They force-feed sex to us. They shove spoonfuls of sex down our open and eager throats. We need it. We crave it. We can barely live without it. We are constantly barraged with sexual stimuli. In our culture, sex is ubiquitous. But, here's the rub: not all of us are having sex on a regular basis. In fact, there are many of us who have never had sex and probably never will, or others who are mired in decades-long monogamous, sexless relationships. And thankfully, for those people, there are strip clubs. I once read a caption in *Vice* magazine's Dos & Don'ts that stated: "If strip clubs were honest about what lay behind their doors…they'd all be named Frustration McLonelys," and I'm at a loss to think of a more fitting appellation.

I've never considered myself to be a "strip club guy." Sure, I'd go for a bachelor party or birthday, but I never frequented a strip club. I've always felt that strip clubs are a waste of money and a needless source of sexual frustration. As a patron, it's rare to get laid at one, unless you're a celebrity or a drug dealer. That being said, on those occasions that I found myself at a strip club, I've always enjoyed the show. For anyone who has not been to a strip club, "the show" typically involves a woman disrobing to two songs and then stepping off the stage and making herself available for private dances. All human beings love exhibition.

From gladiator battles and public executions to rubbernecking an accident and watching reality television, we are all voyeurs at heart. We're intrigued by other people's relationships, their mishaps, and most of all their misfortune. I equate strip clubs with the traveling sideshows of the early twentieth century. However, instead of lobster boy or the bearded woman displaying their grotesque appearance on a wooden stage in the middle of a soiled tent, we have an attractive twenty-year-old woman seductively removing articles of clothing on a brightly lit stage in a lavish nightclub. People attended these freak shows in search of the "other," something that differed from their ordinary lives. Typical strip club regulars rarely associate with beautiful women in their daily lives, let alone see them nude. The strip club is their escape, their gateway to that other world. One may call a visit to the strip club the ultimate fantasy or an erotic escape; but to me, strip clubs are essentially sideshows with young, attractive women in lieu of the monstrous oddities. And I can attest that the line between the two is oftentimes quite blurred.

Since the early twentieth century, a visit to the strip club has been a necessary rite of passage for all American males. Despite its size, every small town in this country either has a local strip club or is within twenty miles of one. And every kid in that town knows exactly where that strip club is located. For me, it was a dilapidated Déjà Vu on a remote exit off I-75 near Saginaw, Michigan. Every Friday night, my family would pass it on our way to the synagogue for Shabbat services, and my twelve-year-old self would stare out the car window, imagining the drug-fueled orgies that went on behind its blackened glass doors. Wistfully, I'd scrutinize the Déjà Vu sign that displayed their logo of crossed legs in fishnet stockings and their curious slogan, "1000s of beautiful girls and 3 ugly ones." The rest of the drive I'd sit in the backseat lost in thought, pondering the meaning of that slogan. Why would they need three ugly girls if there were thousands of beautiful ones? They must have to do special chores, like bathe the beautiful girls or prepare their meals. And how is it possible to fit that many women in such a small building? They must be very tiny women. One time, as my father and I drove past the Déjà Vu, I asked him why they needed three ugly girls when they had so many beautiful ones, and he sternly remarked that I had more important things to think about, like learning how to chant my Torah portion because my bar mitzvah was only a few months away. But I preferred to think about the thousands of tiny, beautiful women in that mysterious pink building. My father was the rabbi of three small congregations in Michigan: Saginaw, Bay City, and Midland, locally known as the Tri-Cities. He'd usually have to head to the synagogue earlier than the rest of us, as he had to set up for the night's service, which meant my mother would drive my sister and me there. On occasion, I'd hitch a ride with my friend Brandon and his perverted father, Dennis. Brandon's parents were divorced, and his father never remarried. He was one of those effeminate dads who spoke with a slight lisp and creeped little kids out. Needless to say, it didn't help much that he was an alcoholic and prone to uttering inappropriate comments. One Friday night, on our way to services, we drove past the Déjà Vu, and Brandon—who was sitting in the front seat while another friend of mine, Daniel, and I sat in the back—asked his dad what went on inside.

"Dad, what goes on in there?" I couldn't believe he asked his dad that question. Sure, we thought about that place all the time, but none of us would have the chutzpah to ask an adult about it. Usually, we'd pretend that we didn't notice the run-down pink building as we drove by. Daniel and I were on the edge of our seats, leaning forward to hear Dennis's answer.

"Which place, son?" he asked casually, knowing full well the building his son was asking about.

"That pink building right there. The Déjà Vu." Brandon pointed to it.

"Oh, that one. Ha. Don't worry about it. You're too young to go in there."

His response was less than satisfying. "What do you mean too young? Why? What goes on in there?"

"Bubbelah, I said you don't want to go there. Jewish boys don't go to places like that."

"Why not? I want to check it out." Brandon was upset that his father called him "Bubbelah" in front of his friends, and I could tell by his grimace that he wasn't about to let this interrogation rest.

"Because there are nasty women in there, okay?" Dennis was getting annoyed. At this point, Daniel and I were captivated, our chins touching the edge of the front seat so we could hear every word.

"What do you mean by nasty? What do they do?"

Dennis frowned and shot a disapproving glance at the two kids leaning forward in the backseat. "If you kids go in there right now, at your age, those women will chop your little penises off," he replied sharply, lisping on the first "s" in "penises."

I was shocked and utterly confounded. We all were. Our young minds were reeling from this revelation. What type of community did we live in that would tolerate an establishment of this sort to exist just outside its borders? It was criminal. Daniel and I sat back in our seats,

46

pondering what this disclosure meant, our minds deluged with unanswered questions. Why would these women want to chop our penises off? What do they do with our penises afterward? Are these women members of a Satanic cult or something?

Yet, Brandon was the skeptic of our group. We had barely driven by the place when he pounded his fist on top of the dashboard and yelled, "Bullshit!" Daniel and I were stunned; never before had we witnessed such audacity. Dennis was also a bit taken aback and suddenly slammed on his brakes and pulled over to the side of the road.

"How dare you say that? Are you questioning me?" he shouted in his effeminate tone, casting a sidelong glance at the two of us in the backseat.

"Dad, I don't believe you. I don't think there are women in there who would do that." Brandon spoke with impressive defiance in his high-pitched preteen voice.

Dennis sat there for a few moments, hands clenching the steering wheel, before suddenly shifting the car into gear and pulling a U-turn across the two-lane highway. He drove towards the Déjà Vu and made a sharp right turn into its graveled parking lot. Daniel and I sat motionless in the backseat, frozen in fear. He put the car in park, shut off the engine, and we sat there in silence for about two or three minutes. I noticed that there were only two other cars in the parking lot. Finally, Dennis let out a protracted sigh, looked over at his son in the passenger seat, and said, "Well then, let's find out." He then turned his head towards Daniel and me in the backseat and asked, "What about you two? Do you guys want to find out what goes on in there?" He had a cruel, sinister grin on his face.

"No, sir, I don't need to know what goes on in there," I said, my voice quavering with fear. Daniel just shook his head.

"Okay. Well, I guess it's just my son and me. Come on, Brandon, let's go." This was the first time I'd heard Dennis speak without any hint of a lisp. He stepped out of the car and slammed the door shut. He then walked over to the passenger side and threw the door open. "Well, what are you waiting for?"

Brandon looked back at his friends in the backseat and mouthed the word "pussy" as he slid out of the passenger seat and exited the vehicle. Dennis grabbed his right elbow and pulled him toward the black glass doors of the faded pink building. Daniel and I stared out the rear window at the two figures making their way across the parking lot. Initially Brandon walked with pride and a sense of defiance, but as they came within twenty feet of the entrance his will started to crumble. It was demoralizing. He began to fall back, yet his father with a vise-like grip on his arm pulled the boy towards the glass doors underneath the pink neon Déjà Vu sign with the letters "e" and "v" burned out. They were about ten feet from the door when Brandon fell to his knees sobbing. His father released the boy's arm and stood there watching his son crying on the ground. After a minute or so, he crouched down and lifted the boy's head up, wiped the tears from his face with his handkerchief, and whispered something to him. To this day, Brandon never told me what he said. The two walked back towards the car, Brandon's dad with his arm wrapped tightly around his son's shoulders. Daniel and I sat in the backseat paralyzed with fear. Dennis floored it out of the parking lot, his Lincoln Continental spraying gravel over the two cars parked behind him, and drove to the synagogue for Shabbat services. For the next hour and a half, I sat in my felt-covered chair not paying the least bit of attention to my father delivering his sermon about the weekly Torah portion. Rather, my thoughts were focused on the demon women who hung out in that mysterious faded pink building waiting to chop my little penis off.

Fast-forward a few years later to junior high. I didn't have to go to services anymore, and my parents would leave me home alone on Friday nights. I'd invite a couple friends over, and we'd steal a bottle of my parents' Manischewitz wine and drink it on the roof of my garage, sharing stories of what we heard happened inside the Déjà Vu strip club, or simply the "Vu" as we called it. We were obsessed with that place. Our primary source of information was my friend Jason's older brother, Brent, who claimed to have received multiple blowjobs on every visit. We truly believed all of Brent's stories because we didn't know any better. In our adolescent minds, we envisioned the inside of the club to be a bacchanalian den of depravity where all of our sexual desires would be fulfilled. It wasn't till ninth grade when I got an opportunity to find out what went on inside the enigmatic Vu. My best friend Kessler came over to my house and shared with me a discovery that transformed our lives. Earlier that day his mother forced him to go to Kmart to get his portrait taken for his grandmother's birthday. While he was watching the photographer struggle in vain to get a toddler to smile, he saw a stack of plastic portrait identification cards lying on the photographer's desk. He pocketed a stack of the cards, took his portrait, and rushed to my house to show me his find.

"Dude, you'll never believe what I have," he said, breathing heavily from running up the staircase to my room. Kessler weighed about 250 pounds in the ninth grade, so running about twenty feet was physically exerting for him, let alone a flight of stairs. When he caught his breath, he reached into the pockets of his black Vision Street Wear jeans and tossed the blue plastic cards on my bed.

I picked one of the cards up and examined it for a few seconds before throwing it back on the bed. "What the fuck is that? A library card?"

"No, man, that's a fucking fake ID."

"Are you serious? It says it's a Kmart portrait identification card. Shitty Kmart photographers use these, so they don't forget a kid's name. That's not a fucking fake ID."

"Yeah, it's a fucking fake ID. Think about it. We might not be able to get into a bar with it, but I bet we could use it to get into the Vu."

He was onto something here. I was skeptical about using it to buy beer, but you only had to be eighteen to get into Déjà Vu. "I don't know. They look pretty shitty."

"All we have to do is put a picture in there, type out our address and date of birth, and we'll be set. The fucking Vu's door guy probably doesn't even look at your ID. He just wants to make sure you have one."

I wasn't convinced. "I dunno, man. A retard would know that this is a Kmart ID. I don't think it's gonna work."

"We might as well fucking try. What's gonna happen? They don't let us in and then we go home. Big deal. We won't know unless we give it a shot."

When it came to pussy or buying drugs, Kessler was a perpetual optimist. He had a point though. We didn't have anything to lose. The worst that could happen was that they threw us out of the place. Maybe knocked us around a bit in the parking lot. But it was worth it to get a few bruises if we were able to see naked breasts for the first time.

"All right. I'm down."

We spent the next three hours trying to make those shitty IDs look as authentic as possible. I used a passport photo for the picture and typed a fake name, address, and birth date using my father's typewriter. My name was Roy Stevens, and the year of my birth was 1971, which made me barely eighteen yet old enough to get into the Vu. I was also from Windsor, Canada, because Kessler felt that the door guys would think our IDs looked strange because they were foreign. After folding it a few times and rubbing it on the driveway to make it look a bit worn, I surveyed my new fake ID and had to admit it looked pretty damn good. It was Saturday night, and my parents let Kessler and Jason sleep over at my house. My room was in the basement and had its own entrance, so it was an easy place to sneak out at night. I helped Kessler type out his address and add the finishing touches to his ID. His looked more credible than mine, but he also looked quite a bit older than me. He was fifteen and already had facial hair. Fat kids always appear older than skinny kids. Jason was also a big kid, weighing in around 200 pounds and 6'2" tall, but he had a youthful face, which always gave away his age. We played Sega Genesis games till my parents went to bed around midnight, and then changed into our club outfits, which consisted of a black dress shirt and a pair of black slacks. It would work to our advantage to look as mature as we could. My plan was to borrow my mom's '89 Chrysler LeBaron and drive to the Vu. Even though I was a year from being able to drive legally, my mom often let me use the car to deliver newspapers on my route, and I was confident behind the wheel. We snuck out of the house in the cover of night, slipped the car into neutral, and pushed it up the driveway and onto the road. Cautiously, I turned the keys in the ignition, and we headed towards the mysterious pink building that we had been waiting so many years to enter. We arrived at the Vu just after 12:30 AM, and I made a sharp left into the gravel parking lot. I had not been in this parking lot since that fateful day with Brandon and his father. After all these years, I was still scared shitless. Though we tried our best not to show it, we were all scared shitless. I shifted the car into park, and we sat there mustering our collective willpower. We listened to The Doors' "Touch Me" playing on the radio as we summoned up the courage to go through with our gambit. Finally, Kessler spoke up.

"Are we going to do this or what?"

"I dunno. They're gonna laugh at these IDs," I replied. Jason sat in the backseat not saying a word.

"We didn't take your mom's car and drive all the way out here just to turn back and head home. We gotta at least try to get in." For better but usually for worse, Kessler was a great motivator.

"Okay, I'm down. Let's go in after this song." I turned the volume up, and we sat listening to Jim Morrisson wail about being touched inappropriately by some woman and thinking that the same thing was in store for us. I stared apprehensively at the neon-lit entrance, wondering how severe our injuries would be when the bouncer tossed us out. The song ended and I shut the car off.

"Let's go."

I exited the car and slammed the door shut. Kessler and Jason slowly clambered out and followed behind me as I strode with purpose towards the pink neon-lit doorway. When I reached the entrance of the Vu, I looked back to make sure that they were still behind me, took a deep breath, and pushed the door open. The air conditioning blasted me with a malodorous mix of cool air, cigarette smoke, disinfectant, and cheap perfume. It caused me to sneeze five times consecutively, and I probably would have continued sneezing had the enormous black man standing in front of me not said, "Goddamn, boy, 'bless you' ten times." Regaining my composure, I muttered a weak "thanks" and checked my shirt to make sure it wasn't covered in mucus. The lobby was also a sex shop, and we surveyed the room in amazement at the vibrators and dildos hanging from the walls, and the bins overflowing with VHS porn movies. I had never seen so much porn. It was overwhelming. I had to steel myself for a few seconds before approaching the fat, frowning cashier with a mullet haircut and a cigarette dangling from the corner of his mouth. His large frame was perched precariously on a stool behind a glass counter, and he was casually flipping through a porn magazine. He looked annoyed, as if he was irritated that we were standing in front of him and now he had to do his job.

"You got an ID? You have to be eighteen to come in here," he said gruffly, lacking emotion.

"Sure. Yes, yes, I do. Hold on one second please." I fumbled around in my pocket for my wallet, pulled out the blue Kmart ID, and shakily handed it to him. "Here."

He passively took it from me, glanced at it for a few seconds, and dropped it on the glass countertop. "Long way from home, huh?"

"Excuse me?" Despite the air conditioning, I could feel that the back of my dress shirt was drenched with sweat.

"I said you're a long way from home. Windsor's about two hours east of here."

"Oh yes. Windsor. Yes. It's far away, but I live here now. I'm in college." It had completely slipped my mind that I had used a Canadian address on the fake ID, but I felt I saved face by saying that I was in college.

The cashier was indifferent. "It's five dollars to get in, and you gotta buy two drinks. And you better tip the girls." He pointed his chubby index finger at me.

"Will do. Thanks." I was so astonished that our gambit worked that my mouth could barely form words. The porno gatekeeper actually believed that I was an eighteen-year-old man from Canada, or more likely, he just didn't care and wanted my five dollars. Behind me, I could hear Kessler and Jason exhale an audible sigh of relief. I quickly paid the man, grabbed my ID off the counter, and slipped it back into my wallet. I was planning to take special care of that ID as it would be quite useful for our many future visits. Kessler and Jason confidently handed the cashier their identification, paid the entrance fee, and we triumphantly marched through the black curtain into the den of iniquity that our adolescent minds had dreamed about for so many years.

Surprisingly, the club was very similar to how Jason's older brother described it. There was a stage in the middle of the room surrounded by chairs and small round tables, and the walls were lined with couches for lap dances. As I grew older, I learned that this is the common design for almost every strip club. It was Saturday night, and the club was packed with guys and half-naked women. We stood there, motionless, for a couple minutes with the curtain open, attempting to mentally process everything. I'm sure we would have stood there longer had the surly cashier not shouted, "Close the fucking curtain!" I released the curtain and immediately came to the realization that we were now "inside the club." I looked over at Kessler and Jason and saw that they were both grinning widely as they came to a similar realization. The club was dark except for the bright, flashing stage lights and the black lights perched above the lap-dance couches. REO Speedwagon blasted from the club's speakers while a naked woman swung from the pole on the middle of the stage. Drooling perverts wearing trucker hats threw dollar bills at her from the front row. Practically every couch in the room had a guy sitting on it with a writhing naked woman on his lap. Four massive television screens displayed porn movies. We stood there mouths agape, trying to absorb it all. It was much better than how Jason's brother described it. We had entered Shangri-La. The DJ turned the volume down and told us to grab a seat in the front row, but we just found the first open table and sat down. This was sensory overload. Our virgin minds could hardly process all the porn, let alone the live naked women dancing before us. We had never even seen a naked woman before. We sat there in silence, our eyes glued on the woman onstage. It took us a minute to notice that there was a bikini-clad waitress standing beside our table, asking us if we wanted to order a drink.

Since no one else seemed to be capable of articulation, I spoke up for the group. "What do you have?"

"We have pop and O'douls," she replied. For those fortunate enough not to be born in Midwestern America, pop is the vernacular term for soda. However, I was in the dark about O'douls.

"What's O'douls?"

"That's non-alcoholic beer." Since the Vu was a fully nude strip club, they were not allowed to serve alcoholic beverages. "Would you like one?"

"Yeah, we'll have three O'douls." I looked at my companions, and they nodded in assent, still unable to peel their eyes away from the naked girl onstage. At the very least, fake beer would make us seem more mature than drinking a coke. She returned in a few minutes with our beverages. Kessler paid her and gave her a five-dollar tip, which really seemed to impress her. We watched the next three girls strip onstage, in silence and with undivided attention that was broken only when an attractive blonde stripper in a neon green bikini sat down at our table.

"Hey, guys, how are you doing tonight?" she asked in a high-pitched, almost Valley Girl inflection.

We looked at the girl desperately, trying not to focus on her massive breasts barely being covered by a miniscule piece of neon green fabric. I was too scared to speak. I didn't even know how to respond. I had never spoken to a woman wearing such little clothing. It was Kessler who finally spoke up before it became exceedingly awkward.

"Ummm. We're doing good. How are you?" he said, his voice only slightly wavering.

She laughed, obviously amused by our anxious behavior. "I'm doing okay. Is this your first time here?"

"Ummm. No, we've been here a couple times before. It's just been a little while."

"Oh, okay. Where are you guys from?"

Jason and I didn't answer her. We just looked at Kessler, who had tacitly been nominated as the table's spokesman. Kessler replied, "We're from Canada originally, but we're here for college." He flashed me a smile when he said this, and I knew he was ridiculing me for saying this earlier.

"Okay, that's cool. Do you guys go to Saginaw Valley State University? I'm taking a couple classes there."

"Ummm. Yeah, that's where we go. I'm studying theater there. They have a wonderful theater department." I didn't know where he was going with this, but it sounded plausible.

"That sounds awesome. Would you like a dance?" she asked, revealing her true motive for sitting at our table and briefly conversing with us.

Kessler bit his lower lip, nervously glanced over at Jason and me for a few seconds, and then back at the blonde stripper with the huge breasts and said, "Yes, yes, I would love a dance." With that, she stood up, grasped his hand, and led him over to an open couch. Jason and I stared at him with trepidation mixed with envy. I couldn't believe we were actually inside this place, let alone my best friend had a naked woman grinding on his lap. We watched him for a song or two before the DJ stopped the music to announce the next performer. He seemed really excited as he said her name, and the crowd erupted into a frenzy of applause as an attractive woman walked onto the stage. She was the feature entertainer of the evening, not a regular dancer. Her name was Porsche Lynn, a popular eighties adult film star. At the time, I had never heard of her, but a couple years later I became well acquainted. A crowd of perverts rushed over to claim seats in the front row. I looked over at Jason and smiled wryly as I stood up and grabbed one of the open seats. Jason soon followed and sat next to me. We both had a stack of dollar bills in front of us and focused our attention on the woman onstage. She danced for a bit, and towards the end of the song, she removed her top and crawled on all fours around the front of the stage. She stopped in front of me and picked up a dollar bill from the table and stuck it in my mouth. She slammed my face into her chest and then, squeezing her breasts together, took the dollar bill from my lips. She used the same maneuver on Jason and on pretty much every guy in the front row before standing up and dancing to the next song. She removed the rest of her outfit and crawled around the stage completely nude. I was so enthralled that I didn't notice Kessler had sat down next to me. He mouthed the words "this is awesome" and threw a handful of singles on the stage. After her performance, we sat down at our table and interrogated Kessler about his lap dance.

"What was it like? Should we get one?" I asked.

"You guys have to get a lap dance. It was the most amazing thing I've ever done."

"How much was it?"

"Twenty bucks for two songs. I got four songs and gave her eighty."

"Can you loan me some money?" I only had about $40.

Kessler gave me $40 and repeated his assertion that we had to get a lap dance. I looked around the room to see if there were any available dancers when a young brunette approached our table. She asked if any of us wanted a lap dance and smiled long enough for me to catch a glimpse of her braces. She couldn't have been more than eighteen years old. I nodded, and she grabbed my hand and led me to an open couch. She sat down next to me while we waited for the current song to finish.

"My name's Michelle. What's yours?"

I was too nervous to remember the name on my fake ID and meekly replied, "David."

"I like the name David. Have you ever been here before?"

"Yeah, a couple times. Why?"

"You seem kinda nervous."

"Ummm. I'm not nervous. It's just that you're really pretty."

She laughed when I said this. "Okay then. Let's have some fun." When the next song started, she removed her top and straddled me. Her breasts seemed small, but I really had little basis of comparison. She grinded on my lap for about a minute before shoving her naked breasts into my face. I was already so excited that when I felt her nipple graze my lips, I ejaculated. I tried to play it off that it didn't happen, but she immediately realized that my pants were wet and jumped off of me.

"What the fuck? That doesn't happen till the second song. Jesus."

"I'm sorry." I was so embarrassed that I didn't know what else to say.

With a look of sheer annoyance, she said, "Just give me $40."

I handed her the money, trying not to make eye contact. She snatched it from my hand and briskly walked away while snapping her top back on. I was left sitting on the vinyl couch alone with a growing wet stain on the crotch of my pants. Not wanting to return to the table, I went to the bathroom and slipped into a stall that reeked of semen and Lysol, and used a wad of toilet paper to wipe away the sticky mess on my crotch. I did the best I could, and then rejoined my friends at the table.

Kessler was the only one at the table, and as soon as I sat down he asked, "How was it?"

"It was good," I replied, trying not to let on that I had just prematurely ejaculated.

"That was quick. Did you blow your load or something?"

"No, it was just a short one. Not a full lap dance."

"Yeah, I totally blew mine within the first minute, but the chick didn't seem to care."

"Really? Yeah, I blew mine too, but my chick flipped out." We both started laughing but I was still embarrassed. Jason eventually returned to the table after having a similar experience. We didn't bother to ask as his self-satisfied smirk said it all. It was almost 2:00 AM, and we had to leave. On our way out, we noticed that Porsche Lynn was posing for pictures. Since it only cost $10, Kessler insisted that we have our picture taken with her. She said for $20 she'd do a group photo, so I sat in the middle of my two friends, and she straddled us all stark naked with her legs spread open. The whole time I was worried that she was going to feel my damp crotch and freak out, but I imagine that's an occupational hazard in her profession. Her photographer handed us a Polaroid, and now we held indisputable, tangible evidence of the night's events. We exited the pink neon doorway with our heads held high and our crotches damp, and we rode back in silence the entire drive home thinking about the miraculous experience that we had shared.

The following Monday we showed up at school not as fifteen-year-old boys but as fifteen-year-old men. We told everyone about our weekend exploits and shared the marvels of our experience. But our fellow classmates didn't believe us. Despite our claims and assertions, they were filled with skepticism, that is, until I reached into the back pocket of my jeans and produced the Polaroid of the three of us with a naked porn star. Their jaws simultaneously dropped to the ground as they stared at the photograph of the naked Porsche Lynn with her legs spread open on our laps. We were the most popular kids in our grade for about two weeks when one of us slipped and told them how we procured our fake IDs. That afternoon, a score of high school kids showed up at Kmart to get their own portrait identification cards. The next time we tried to get into the Vu, the cashier told us to "fuck off" and pointed at the door, but it didn't matter because we had already conquered that place.

The Bigger the Bills, the Bigger the Thrills

The strip club DJ is required to provide the dancer, regardless of the amount of her tip, with an introduction, two songs about three minutes in length, a light show, and a request from the crowd for a departing round of applause at the end of her set. Since most customers pay little or no attention to the man on the microphone, I'd say music selection is the most important aspect of the job. But, at this moment, I want to give credence to the abrupt utterances, the directions, the jargon, the amusing one-liners, and the inane prattle of the strip club DJ. Next time you visit a strip club, try not to focus all of your attention on the bouncing breasts before you and take a brief moment to listen to the DJ's incoherent babble. I use the term "incoherent" because most strip club DJs are barely audible over the music playing through the club's sound system. The characteristic muffled vocal prompts customers to sarcastically remark that all strip club DJs sound the same. My first reaction is to dismiss this as an ignorant generalization, but it is somewhat valid. Strip clubs tend to use cut-rate soundboards with built-in voice compressors giving the DJ a tacky, vulgar intonation that sounds more fitting for a monster truck rally or an air show than a gentlemen's club:

"Sunday, Sunday, Sunday at the Boobie Bungalow, gentlemen, move up to the tip rail and get ready to see some prime ass and titty action."

61

The reason the cheesy voice seems to fit is because, in essence, strip clubs are cheesy. Perhaps it's me, but watching a girl dance naked to a Whitesnake song while some fat, balding guy sitting next to you has a rolled-up dollar bill hanging from his mouth and his face buried between some girl's massive bosom is cheesy. Regardless of how you attempt to justify it, stripping is not a highbrow art form; and don't bring up burlesque, because modern-day burlesque dancers are just strippers who are too fat, tattooed, and old to work at a real strip club. At most clubs, the DJ is not allowed to perform a stand-up routine and is instructed to say as little as possible. However, we do throw in the occasional one-liners, ridicule the perverts, and playfully mock the dancers. What we are permitted to say over the mic depends largely on the attitude of the management. At the Doll House and other lower-tier clubs I've worked at, I had a lot more freedom behind the mic; but at the upscale clubs, it was required to maintain a level of professional decorum. Some managers prefer the DJ to simply announce the dancer's name for her stage show and advertise the dinner or drink specials once an hour. Their philosophy is that the show is about the girls, not the DJ, and customers do not frequent a strip club to listen to a blathering half-wit who can hardly be heard over the music. While most DJs repeat the same tried-and-true lines, I always strived to inject some originality into my lines. My enthusiasm for a dancer's introduction was based on two factors: how well I knew the girl and how well she tipped me. When a DJ works at a club longer than three months, it's inevitable that he will get to know some of the girls on a personal level. He learns specific details about their lives, such as where they're from, their modeling careers, their porn aspirations, their favorite television shows, preferred sexual positions, etc. If I liked the girl who was about to walk onstage, I would be sure to point out her specific accomplishments or other noteworthy endeavors. For example, I became good friends with a stripper named Natasha who had a successful modeling career outside of the industry. When she took the stage I'd give her an elaborate introduction by announcing:

"Gentlemen, you've seen her on the cover of *Maxim* magazine, she recently did a spread for *Stuff*, now check her out live on the Ruby Club's center stage. Give it up, boys! This is Natasha."

I gave a great introduction to a girl named Raven who had posed for several adult magazines during her ephemeral porn career. I liked Raven because she was a rocker chick who always danced to ACDC and loved strobe lights. Before she walked onstage, I'd announce something like:

"Gentlemen, I hope you're ready to rock and roll, cuz our next entertainer is gonna rock your fucking world. You've seen her in *Penthouse*. You've seen her in *Cheri*. You've seen her in your wet dreams. Live at the Ruby Club. Give it up for Raven."

Then I'd hit the strobe lights till at least two pervs in the front row had a seizure. I found it amusing to draw attention to the porn magazines that the dancers had been featured in. The name of the magazine would immediately capture the attention of every customer in the room and prompt them to move to the front row, or "erection section" as we referred to it. Though it was rare, some girls possessed an ironic sense of humor, and for them, I'd fabricate porn magazines that they had been featured in.

"Gentlemen, straight out of the pages of *Black Tail* magazine. Fellas, put those hands together, the very beautiful Alizé for your pleasure."

"Fellas, you might have seen her spread in *Barely Legal*. Well, now's your chance to check her out live onstage. Give it up for Roxie."

Not only did I have a personal relationship with these dancers, they tipped me quite well, so it was in my best interest to provide them with an elaborate introduction. Conversely, I'd reserve my standard introduction for the dancers that did not tip me or for the ones that I didn't like. My standard "intro" consisted merely of a dancer's stage name and request for applause. One of the greatest opportunities for a strip club DJ to sling some quality cheese is when customers are not tipping the dancer onstage. As a personal rule, I rarely spoke during a dancer's performance. I felt that it interfered with their stage show and, quite honestly, no one really cared what I had to say. My only exception to this rule was when the stage was barren of dollar bills. At any strip club, it's imperative that customers tip the dancer onstage. By throwing a few dollars on the stage, customers show their appreciation to the girl getting naked and demonstrate their interest in that dancer. At every club I worked at, when the crowd is not tipping, the DJ is allowed to openly deride them. The extent of the derision depends on the management of the club. At the Doll House, the DJ was basically uncensored. Management would even allow us to spotlight the non-tipping customers and ridicule them directly. At the Ruby Club and other upper-tier venues I've worked at, I was allowed to mention tipping but not in a discourteous manner. I would closely watch a few dancers' stage shows and note how many tips she received. It's not like I was expecting a customer to "make it rain" every time a girl took the stage, but at least they could throw a few dollar bills up there. If there were only a couple dollars on the stage and a large crowd present, I would coax them to start tipping by repeating these innocuous lines:

"Gentlemen, I know you didn't come all the way to the Doll House to hang out with a bunch of dudes. Move on up to that front row and find out why we call it the 'erection section.'"

"The bigger the bills, the bigger the thrills. It's time to move on up to the erection section and party with that pussy."

"Gentlemen, you provide the greenery and I'll give you the scenery. Let's work together here."

"Fellas, let's get some tips up on that stage. These girls are working hard to keep you hard. So show a little love out there tonight."

"Gentlemen, think about it this way: If you were getting naked on that stage, these girls would tip you, and they would tip you real good."

"Gentlemen, don't be shy. These girls aren't going to bite. If they do, they'll bite you in all the right places. Move up to the front row and take care of this sexy lady."

Now if these lines went unheeded and the girls were still not being tipped, I'd become much more vengeful and personal with my remarks. That's when I'd focus one of the club's spotlights on individuals and groups of non-tippers and ruthlessly mock them in front of the dancers. Turning the volume of the music down to near silence, I'd announce:

"Hey, I want to take this moment to talk to the sausage fest in the back over there. What are you guys doing in the strip club tonight? Is it your first time? Are you strip club virgins? Let me clue you in on a strip club custom. When guys go to strip clubs, they tip the girls and buy one or two lap dances. So far, you guys have done neither. Real men don't sit in the back of the club and play with each other's ball sacks. So gentlemen, let's join the team here and show a little appreciation tonight. You can play with each other's balls at home."

The higher I got, the more creative I'd become, especially if the drug of choice that night was methamphetamine.

"Gentlemen, it's time to worship at the altar of the vulva. Step on up to the front row, put a dollar bill in your mouth, and let's praise the blessed vulva."

"Gentlemen. The bigger the bills, the bigger the thrills. Give a little, get a lot. I know that dollar bill is burning a hole in your pocket. Put it this way. Once you start tipping, I'll shut the fuck up. And I know everyone wants that."

"Gentlemen, in the corner over there. This is God. That's right. The Supreme Being. Tonight I'm feeling wrathful, and I'm rather displeased with your behavior here at the Doll House. You have not tipped a single lady tonight, nor have you purchased a lap dance. Let me ask you some simple questions: What the fuck did you come here for? Do you know how I feel about sodomy? I don't like it. Move up to the fucking tip rail and show some generosity to these young ladies before I strike you down with a lightning bolt, a flood, or AIDS or something."

The most egregious offender was the customer seated in the front row, or "erection section," and not tipping the girl directly before them. Not only was this offensive to the girl onstage, it was an affront to me as well. This particular breed of miserly bastard received no mercy. I made it my mission to shame this man until he threw a couple dollars onstage or hastily exited the club. And I always busted out the spotlight for them.

"This is for the dude in the red hat in the front row: Not tipping in the front row is like going through a drive thru and not ordering any food. It makes absolutely no sense. Get some tips on the stage or move to the back of the room."

"Gentlemen, we call that area at the front of the stage the tip rail for a reason. That is where you place tips for the dancer onstage. The no-tipping seats are in the back of the club. So if you're not going to tip the lady, move to the asshole seats in the back of the club and let a generous man have your seat in the front row."

Or, sometimes, I would make it a direct, personal attack:

67

"Hey, fat guy in the flannel shirt with the shitty haircut. You are seated at the tip rail, which means you should be tipping the dancer onstage. If you are not going to tip her, move your fat ass to the back of the club and let someone who is going to tip have your seat. Thank you. And do yourself a favor, when you go back to Wisconsin, lay off the Doritos, man. Jesus, your pants must hate you."

While these comments were entertaining, they sometimes had serious consequences for the club's security. I've been the instigator of several altercations, and had it not been for the bouncers and, on one occasion, a couple dancers, I would have had my ass severely kicked. One Saturday night at the Doll House, I mercilessly derided a group of six or seven guys who had been at the club for over two hours and had not spent any money tipping the dancers or buying private shows. I did the spotlight thing and said:

"Hey, this is for the group of guys in the back: Quit making out with your boyfriend and party with the pussy on the main stage. I know we're in San Francisco, but you guys are in a fucking strip club. Jesus Christ. This isn't the cock and ball show. You guys should be at a leather bar in the Castro. You'd have more fun."

From working at the lower-tier clubs, I've learned that random homophobic insults tend to inspire fellow patrons to participate in the mockery and ultimately influence the ridiculed party to start tipping in order to save face. In this case, the audience laughed at the group, and one guy started screaming, "Yeah. Faggots. Party with the pussy." The collective mockery angered the group, and one outspoken member took it upon himself to begin heckling me. Hecklers are a common occurrence in strip clubs, in particular the ones that serve alcohol. They are usually intoxicated meatheads whose fragile sexual identities have just been questioned by the DJ, and not only are the other customers laughing at them, the girls are laughing at them as well. Their pride has just been damaged, and they are upset; their only recourse is to focus their aggression on the source of the derision: the DJ. In this case, the heckler screamed obscenities at both the dancers and me. Every time I would ask the crowd to give a round of applause, the heckler would yell, "Fuck you. You suck. These bitches are ugly." His constant interruptions were annoying and pushed me to up the ante. I turned the music all the way down, focused the spotlight on the offender, and used one of my favorite heckler lines:

"Excuse me, ladies and gentlemen. This is for the loud homosexual in the back over there. I don't come to your work and slap the dick out of your mouth, so would you kindly shut the fuck up and let the girls dance. There are some guys here who want to see some titties tonight. Am I right?"

The entire room erupted into laughter and applause. Even a few of the heckler's companions were laughing at him. The heckler, however, did not appreciate the comment, and he along with three of his friends rushed the booth. They were large meatheads, much larger than myself, and I predicted that I was on the brink of getting my ass kicked. Fortunately, the booth was located in the front of the club next to a large concentration of club security who immediately tackled my assailants.

The fracas quickly turned into a melee with customers, managers, dancers, and security fighting each other. The heckler somehow got past security, grabbed my shirt with his left hand, and started pummeling me with his right. I slipped out of his grip and kicked him as hard as I could in the crotch. He fell to the ground and was stunned for a couple of seconds, allowing me enough time to scramble out of the booth and head outside of the club. When a fight breaks out in the club, the bouncers force the troublemakers outside and beat them on the sidewalk so as to avoid any excessive property damage. There must have been about twenty people fighting in front of the Doll House that night. I stood at a safe distance across the street, smoking a cigarette with a couple dancers. We watched the chairs, tables, fists, stilettos, chunks of hair and teeth fly through the air. It was a fleeting moment of tremendous violence. Within minutes, the cops soon arrived on the scene and quickly stopped the fracas. The ne'er-do-wells were subdued, handcuffed, and lined up against the wall in the alley, and slowly but surely everyone's adrenaline levels returned to normal. The guy who attacked me lay on his stomach with a cop's knee in his back. His face was bloodied, and he cursed at the top of his lungs as I walked by:

"I'm going to fucking kill you, motherfucker. Fuck you. Fuck you. Fuck you. You're fucking dead."

I gave him a wink and a smile as I walked through the torn curtains back into the club. Thankfully, I never saw that man again. Violent brawls were commonplace at the lower-tier clubs I worked at. In fact, there was at least one fight almost every night of the week at the Doll House. I never fought unless it was a matter of self-defense. And in those isolated incidents, I'd do my best to kick my assailant in the balls and run away and hide like an abused housewife. Since the club's management didn't provide their employees with benefits or insurance of any kind, I would have to pay my own medical bills. And needless to say, my damaged pride was not worth a broken nose.

The Ghost of Strip Club DJ Future

Like every other strip club DJ, my lines are not completely my own. Whether we admit it or not, we all "borrow" from each other, especially when we're first embarking on this fruitful career. But there are certain fundamental lines that all of us must employ to keep the show running smoothly. For example, the DJ has to know how to direct the girls to the proper stages, or they will have no idea where to go. If he fails to announce their stages correctly, the dancers will wander about in a morass of confusion due to their inherent lack of common sense and the fact that most are stoned or drunk during their entire shift. The stage rotation is specific to the club and can only be learned by paying close attention to a more experienced DJ. Novice emcees should hang out at other local clubs and steal lines from their DJs. I visited at least four or five different local clubs, listened closely, and lifted a bevy of lines. I then tweaked them somewhat to fit my style and make it less obvious that they were stolen. It's perfectly acceptable to steal lines from DJs at other clubs, but it's verboten to steal lines from a DJ at your own club, in particular from a seasoned DJ. This is because the dancers will listen to you parroting the other DJ's lines, and, always willing to create unnecessary drama, they will promptly inform him of the infraction. And even worse than losing your credibility, you'll most likely be accosted by the peeved strip club DJ veteran and receive a stern lecture about stealing lines. I've seen this happen many times.

When I worked at the Ruby Club, there were four DJs on rotation: Tommy, Ryan, Larry, and myself. Tommy and I worked the night shifts, and Ryan and Larry, who were less experienced, worked the days. Ryan had to be one of the least creative people I'd ever met, not to mention the worst emcee that I had ever encountered. He was a tall, thin man in his mid-thirties, with buzz-cut hair that he shaved himself and a mouthful of rotten teeth. Ryan had recently moved to San Francisco from somewhere in the Midwest, and one could immediately discern from his dead-eyed expression and the irritating way he slowly sucked air in and out of his open mouth with each breath that he had huffed his fair share of aerosol products throughout his formative years. I don't think Ryan had graduated from high school, and he would evade the question when I brought it up. Although he claimed to not use any drugs, Ryan seemed like he was in a perpetual state of "high" at all times. Our interactions were limited, as we only saw each other for ten minutes or so during shift change. And our typical conversation involved his endless queries about whether or not I'd "fuck that bitch onstage." While I set up for my shift, Ryan sat on a bar stool by the soundboard, slowly smoking a cigarette and staring at me. Eventually, he'd signal for my attention, point to the girl dancing on the main stage, and ask in his laidback stoner drawl, "Would you fuck that bitch?"

Humoring him, I'd survey the dancer for a few seconds and respond, "I suppose it'd be more fun than jerking off. Yes, I would."

He'd burst into laughter as if I had told the funniest joke he had ever heard, and once his laughter deteriorated into sporadic chuckles, he'd say, "I wouldn't fuck her with your dick," and start laughing again. We'd repeat the same routine two or three more times until my shift started. That joke never became stale for him, but it always confused me. How could he gain control of my genitalia? Was he telekinetic? I never questioned him though. Rather, I'd smile and nod, deftly avoiding further conversation. He sometimes spoke about how many clubs he had worked at in his hometown and that it was "bullshit" that he didn't have any night shifts. He carried on about his years of experience, but I had never met a DJ with less style and originality. He had only been working there for a month or two when I—along with half of the dancers—noticed that Ryan was making good use of Tommy's signature lines. Not just a few scattered lines here and there; he was using every single one of them. It was as if he had written them down and recited them like an actor does the lines of his script. At first, I was a bit hurt because I always thought that I slung some decent lines, undeniably better than Tommy's trite prattle, but apparently, they weren't good enough for Ryan. However, upon further consideration, I came to the conclusion that it was a good thing he wasn't stealing my lines because I didn't want to have to give him the lecture. In fact, I didn't even know the lecture well enough to give it.

To put it mildly, Tommy was enraged when he caught wind of the pilfering of his lines. Tommy was very proud of his status as senior DJ of the club and was overly protective of his "sacred lines," which is exactly how he referred to them. Personally, I thought Tommy sounded like the dirty old man that he was, but he said it took him years to perfect his style. At the time of this writing, Tommy had been working in the industry for about eighteen years, and it's understandable the reason his lines were sacred. His lines were all he had. Tommy was a thrice-divorced forty-seven-year-old man with a huge gut, a greasy mullet ponytail, and arms covered in faded pin-up girl tattoos. Outside of the club, I never saw him wear anything other than a faded Chicago Bears jersey and stained sweatpants. Tommy was as close to the stereotype of a strip club DJ as one can get. I used to consider him "the ghost of strip club DJ future." Not only did he have the trademark horrendous teeth, he was also a recovering alcoholic and meth addict. The highlight of Tommy's life was the late eighties when he used to roadie for Faster Pussycat. He lived in Hollywood back then, and as he would attest whenever someone mentioned eighties hair metal, "Those were the fuckin' days, man. Back then I wore the cuntboots." He definitely did not wear the cuntboots anymore. Those cuntboots had been buried under a filthy mattress filled with shame, regret, and failure. Honestly, I don't think Tommy had been laid in the past ten years without paying for it. One of my fondest memories of Tommy involved an interaction between him and Lauren, one of the club's house moms. The house moms essentially served as liaisons between the dancers and management. Lauren was noticeably pregnant at the time but still worked a shift every now and then. One night Tommy dropped by the club to pick up some of his CDs, noticed Lauren chatting with me, and looked her over a couple times before interrupting our conversation.

"Fuckin' pregnant, huh?"

Lauren nodded and forced a thin smile. None of the house moms liked Tommy. There wasn't much about him to like. Continuing this unwelcome conversation, he inquired, "So, you have to go out and buy new clothes and shit?"

Without answering his inane question, she waved goodbye to me and hastily exited the booth. Tommy was taken aback.

"What the fuck crawled up her ass? You know I never liked pregnant bitches. They're all fuckin' stuck up and shit."

I laughed uncontrollably for about ten minutes, and when I finally composed myself, I said, "You should write a book."

"About what?" he asked, eyeing me warily. Tommy was always suspicious of being made a fool of, which stemmed from his distrust of anyone with a college education.

"About dealing with pregnant women."

"Why? They're all bitches. I don't want to fucking deal with them."

"Nevermind. Forget I said anything."

Our conversations typically revolved around Tommy telling me stories of the strip club days of yore. Beyond that, we had little to say to each other. When I first started at the club, he told me that I could listen to him "perform," but he better not catch me using his lines or "my ass will be grass." His admonition was good enough for me because I thought his lines were crap. When he found out that Ryan had been stealing his lines, he came to me first.

"Hey, bro, I heard some fucked-up shit the other day. That new guy is using my lines. Do you know anything about that?" I could tell by his furrowed brow that he was really bothered.

I responded diplomatically, trying to avoid being ensnared within the drama. "You know, I might have heard him using lines that sounded like yours, but I don't know for sure. I don't really pay much attention to him."

Tommy then queried both the management and the house moms who confirmed that Ryan was indeed making good use of his "sacred lines." He decided to find out for himself and took time out of his busy schedule to visit the club on a day shift and listen to Ryan on the mic. Regrettably, I wasn't there to witness this incident and had to rely on the eyewitness account of Ashlee, one of the other house moms. She said that Tommy's face contorted into a bitter grimace as he heard his lines being desecrated. It proved too much for him to bear, and he bounded upstairs to the DJ booth, grabbed the back of Ryan's head, and slammed his face into the wall. Though he was stunned for a few seconds, Ryan quickly recovered and pushed Tommy off of him.

"What the fuck, man? Why'd you do that?" he screamed, checking to see if his nose was broken.

"Motherfucker, you're using my fucking lines."

"Why don't you fuck off, you fat bitch?"

This flippant remark pushed Tommy to the breaking point, and he grabbed Ryan by his neck, smashed his face into the wall a couple more times, and attempted to throw him over the railing. Ryan frantically clutched the brass railing with his right hand and feebly attempted to fend off Tommy's blows with his left. The whole time, Tommy kept screaming: "I'll come right through your fucking teeth."

Ashlee said the fight only lasted a couple minutes before two managers and a bouncer pulled Tommy off poor Ryan. Tommy's bloated face was bright red, and he was breathing so heavily that everyone thought that he was about to have a heart attack. Ryan, on the other hand, was clutching his bleeding nose and screaming about suing him, the managers, the club, and anyone who didn't intervene. They suspended Tommy for two weeks, and as fate would have it, Ryan ended up going to jail for domestic battery and never returned to the club. The moral of this story is that a DJ should really try to use his own lines.

The Red Light Special

Aside from the money and frequent sex, ridiculing customers had to be the third most attractive feature of the job. Over time, spinning records at a strip club becomes tedious, and eventually a DJ must search for new and creative ways to amuse himself. I never tired of ridiculing the perverted patrons. At the Doll House and several other lower-tier clubs I worked at, one of the best times to mock customers was during the dance specials that we had to run every half hour. Most strip clubs offer dance specials that encourage customers to buy lap dances. And these specials are quite effective in making money for the club. More often than not, seasoned customers would wait until we ran a dance special because they felt that they were getting more for their money. Since the owner of the club typically takes a percentage of the dancers' private dances, it's imperative that the club has a high lap-dance count for every night shift. In fact, at most clubs, the DJ is evaluated based on the number of dances he sells during his shift, and when he is underperforming he will lose his night shifts. It was one of the more stressful jobs I've ever had. I never knew whether or not I'd be fired or demoted that evening. It always amused me that management considered it to be the DJ's fault that customers weren't purchasing lap dances, as if we had telepathic powers that compelled patrons to waste their money on lap dances. At the Doll House, the owner forced the girls to charge twenty dollars per lap dance of which half went directly to the house. He even hired employees who kept track of the girl's dances so that he'd know exactly how much she owed the house at the end of her shift. In his small, sadistic mind, the best way to keep the dance count as high as possible was to run a Red Light Special every half hour.

The dancers and the DJs despised these specials, but regardless, they boosted lap-dance counts and consequently earned more money for the club. They were aptly titled because of the flashing red lights located in the four corners of the room that the DJ had to switch on prior to announcing the special. The majority of the specials consisted of a 2-for-1 dance or occasionally, a 3-for-1 lap dance. For the unaccustomed, a 2-for-1 dance meant that the customer purchased the first dance, and the second one was on the house. Though the dancers disliked giving a free lap dance, the songs for the specials were a bit shorter than the songs for regular dances, and quite often, the customer would remain upstairs with the girl and continue to buy dances after the special had ended.

Personally, I detested the Red Light Specials because they disrupted the continuity of the show. It takes a while for the DJ to connect with the audience, and as soon as I'd establish a connection, a manager would call on the radio and tell me to run a special after the next song. Then, I'd begrudgingly flip on the flashing red lights and summon all the dancers to line up by the main stage for the Red Light Special. But what I despised most about the specials was the god-awful music that we were required to play from the club's ESPN Jock Jams compilations. If you've ever been to a professional sporting event, you've been subjected to that wretched music: "Who Let the Dogs Out" by Baha Men, or "Whoomp There It Is" by Tag Team, or "Jump Around" by House of Pain, or the most vomit-inducing of them all, "Unbelievable" by EMF. Years have passed, but the memory of that music still makes me cringe. The club owned the entire set of Jock Jams compilations and ordered the DJ to play a couple tracks to pump up the crowd as they watched the dancers walk in a single-file line up the stairs onto the main stage. Once the entire gaggle of strippers were all onstage, they'd turn around and face the crowd, smile, and clap their hands along to the beat of "Whoomp There It Is." And I'd announce in my loudest and most enthusiastic monster truck rally voice:

"Gentlemen, it's time for a Red Light Special right here at the hottest hot spot in town, San Francisco's own Doll House. Guys, check out all these beautiful ladies ready to please you, ready to tease you, ready to rock your world. Ladies, how you doin' tonight?"

The dancers were conditioned to scream excitedly at the utterance of the last phrase and then hastily exit the stage. As they were leaving, I'd announce, still in my hyper-enthused monster truck rally voice:

"Gentlemen, all of these beautiful women are stepping off that stage and available for a 2-for-1 lap dance. It doesn't get any better than this. You buy the first dance, and the second one is on the house. That's right. You heard me correctly. Two dances for the price of one right now and right now only. Take advantage while you can. Your wet dreams have come true tonight. A butt-naked lady on your lap for two songs for the price of one. Double the fun with a 2-for-1. Fuck yeah. Let's do this, fellas. Partner up, couple up with the lady of your choice, and get yourself a 2-for-1 lap dance."

The dancers made their way through the room asking customers if they'd like to take advantage of the special. Most of the customers would head upstairs and buy a 2-for-1 lap dance. Like a sordid version of a high school Sadie Hawkins dance, it always amused me watching the pervert and the stripper walk hand-in-hand on their way towards the lap-dance booths. However, there were always some miserly customers who chose not to participate in the 2-for-1 and preferred to wait it out for the next dancer to come onstage. My General Manager, Joe, told me that I should have no mercy for these "deadbeats." When I started at the Doll House, Joe micromanaged my specials and would leave the back office to watch me perform them. He leaned on the booth smoking a menthol cigarette and offered his unwelcome critique.

"Sanchez, your specials suck major ass. I wouldn't buy a fucking dance from you. It sounds like you're selling fucking magazines. Sell some whores, not magazines. Fuck. At least act like you care, asshole."

Joe was exactly who you'd picture to manage a shitty strip club. He was a tall and thin, uneducated, mustachioed misogynist who had been to prison more than once for domestic violence. Though I think he was originally from Indiana, he affected a southern accent and would tell me in his faux redneck drawl that I needed to get "fucking pumped" for the specials. In his opinion, the specials were the DJ's moment to prove his self-worth to the management. As much as I hate to admit it, he had a point. My specials did "suck ass." I thought the whole charade lacked purpose. There I was, a college graduate who recently lost my high-paying dotcom job, putting a gaggle of strippers on a stage for a lap-dance special. It was demeaning to the women and to myself. In my mind, I could picture my father, the rabbi, frowning in disappointment as he watched his son—who should have been a lawyer or a doctor—

auction off hookers for hapless perverts. But my attitude changed after about a couple months of working there. It was either out of boredom or, more likely, economic necessity, but I started having ironic fun with the specials. I affected a mock zeal to my voice and really got into it. Whenever a manager would tell me to run a special, I eagerly flipped on the red lights and acted like I was auctioning Rembrandts at Sothebys, even though, in actuality, it was more like Frazettas at a garage sale. Soon, I sold more dances than any of the other DJs, and due to my high dance counts, I was promoted to night shifts. In time, I earned Joe's respect, and instead of critiquing my performance, he stood proudly by the booth and derided the customers who refused to participate.

"Sanchez, that was a damn fine special. It really was. You had me convinced. But still, look at those motherfuckers sitting there. Fucking cocksucking faggots." Joe's face was contorted with deep disdain, and I could tell he was genuinely upset. "What the fuck is wrong with you people? You don't like women? What the fuck?"

With his elbow perched upon my shoulder, he told me in earnest that they weren't cooperating because they were "fucking homos." He really believed that. A man could have no legs and be physically unable to walk to the lap-dance booths, but if he didn't at least try to crawl, he was immediately branded a "faggot" in Joe's mind.

"Man, they don't even know the taste of pussy. Probably never even seen one," he said with disgust.

His tone gradually changed as he became more riled. His eyes scanned the room and he shook his head in complete and utter disgust. With his elbow still perched upon my shoulder, he looked me in the eye and said, "These motherfuckers aren't team players. Look at 'em. They would rather sit with their dicks in their hands on the goddamn sidelines than get on the field and play ball. Fuck 'em. You should have no fucking mercy for them because God has no fucking mercy for them. Fucking faggots."

Well, since I now had Joe's consent, I could basically say anything I wanted to the customers who didn't buy a 2-for-1 dance. It was liberating and afforded me the opportunity to infuse some creativity with my derision:

"Gentlemen. What's up with this? You came here to party with pussy, not with the balls. These ladies are moist, wet, and waiting for you. And you. And you over there with the purple shirt. So let's get this party started. Move away from the balls and towards the pussy. Buy a 2-for-1 dance while you can."

I'd wait thirty seconds or so, and if they still refused to buy a dance I'd continue:

"Gentlemen. There's a half-naked woman right in front of you who wants to treat you to a private encounter, and you're saying no. Seriously, take a step back and look at yourself. You are refusing to party with a half-naked woman. Now, I'm no psychiatrist, but in my opinion, you might be gay. You're choosing to hang out with a bunch of dudes instead of a beautiful naked lady. Yes, you could very well be gay."

And for the Spanish speaking patrons:

"Amigos, juega con la penocha. Dos baila privados para uno. Muevete de los huevos y al entra la penocha. Si no compras un baila privado, tu eres maricon."

After a significant amount of ribbing, most customers either found a girl or simply caved to the one pulling on their arm, and headed upstairs for the special. The customers who still refused to participate were punished by having to stare at an empty stage for two songs while the staff scrubbed off the heel marks, disinfected the poles, and wiped the fingerprints off the mirrored walls. I particularly enjoyed taunting the penny-pinching perverts who were sitting there watching the empty stage. During the two-song special, I'd select two painfully slow, sentimental songs such as Neil Diamond's "Love on the Rocks" followed by Journey's "Faithfully," or Foreigner's "I Want to Know What Love Is" paired with practically anything by Air Supply. In my opinion, the stage maintenance was an isolated moment in the space-time continuum where a group of men could be alone in a strip club devoid of women for exactly six minutes. And to make a beautiful situation even more sublime, this group of men was listening to Barry Manilow's "Mandy." Regrettably, most members of the group were bored by the music or the absence of naked women and would shamefully leave the club, but there were always a few stalwarts who steadfastly sat there and stared at that empty stage until the two songs came to an end. It was for them that I made the stage maintenance an introspective, deep soul-searching, meditative male-bonding experience for us all.

"Gentlemen, look at your neighbor and move closer to him. No empty seats. Come on. Move over and sit next to the lonely soul on your right or that crazy cat on your left. It's sharing time." Barry was singing something about a man crying in a window.

"Fellas, for the next seven minutes, it's just me, you, and Barry Manilow. There are no women here to tempt us. To distract us from eachother. It's just us guys. The fellas. Hanging out. Let's make the most of this experience." We had reached the chorus where Barry laments sending his lover away.

"Fellas, that's pretty much what happened here tonight. In this room. These ladies came to you, and they wanted to give you something special, and you sent them away. Think about it. Why didn't we purchase a 2-for-1 lap-dance special? What stopped us?" Now we were at the point of the song where Barry realizes how much he needed Mandy in his life.

"Gentlemen, I don't know why you didn't buy a private dance. I may never know. But what I do know is that all of us in this room could have had a beautiful, fully nude woman on our lap for two songs for the price of one. But no. She's not on your lap, is she? No, she's not. She's on another man's lap right now. And who do we have to blame for that? No one but ourselves."

I'd go on like this until Joe called on the radio and yelled, "Shut the fuck up right now, or you'll be fired. And turn this shit off. Jesus Fucking Christ." But sometimes, Joe wasn't paying attention or was outside smoking a cigarette or shoving a slice of pizza in his mouth while screaming at a dancer about her "piss-poor" attitude, and I continued my unwelcome harangue until the 2-for-1 Red Light Special had come to an end and it was time to put the next dancer onstage.

.

The Blowjob Adventures of Dr. Fellatio

During my five years in the industry, I worked at many clubs throughout the city, but one I recall fondly was a small club called Foxys located downtown in the bowels of San Francisco's infamous Tenderloin district. I liked Foxys for two reasons: it was walking distance from my apartment, and it claimed to be a porno theater as well as a strip club. Foxys had a small projector that displayed pornographic films on a stained 6' x 6' screen hanging on the back wall just above the soda fountain machine. It was mandatory that porn was playing during the hours of operation. From the moment we opened our doors at noon till we closed the club at 2:00 AM, ass-slamming, cum-splattering porn had to be playing on the screen the entire time. Foxys was the only place I've worked where management required the employees to watch pornography. In fact, we would be seriously reprimanded and threatened with termination if there was no porn playing when the General Manager slipped in for a surprise visit.

Prior to my strip club career, I was an avid consumer of pornography. While I appreciated porn on an artistic level, I primarily utilized it as a medium for intense self-discovery and to introduce my girlfriends to the wonderful and exciting world of bisexuality. Like any fist-bumping, beer-drinking American, porn played an integral role in my life. That is until I worked at a strip club. Foxys ruined porn for me. My gradual desensitization to porn was akin to losing a relative to a terminal illness. It was a measured and emotionally heart-wrenching process that

89

was strangely much more tragic than my desensitization to watching the dancers get naked. That made perfect sense to me. I worked with the same ten girls almost every shift. Initially, the sight of their nude bodies swinging on a pole was stimulating and somewhat distracting, but over time, I grew accustomed to their naked flesh, and for the most part, I wasn't even all that attracted to them in the first place. Pornography, conversely, is always exciting; especially in the era of the Internet. If you have a decent online connection, it's virtually impossible to become familiarized with porn. With a few simple keystrokes—no pun intended—one has immediate access to every imaginable genre: new actors, new scenarios, new positions, new stories. Porn was always exciting until I was forced to watch it eight hours a day, five days a week. Anything consumed to the point of excess will become tedious and ultimately repellant. And sadly this was the case for me. My beloved porn, my secret lover, had transformed into the Discovery Channel. It ceased to be arousing or stimulating in any way. It completely lost its effect on me. I soon realized that I stood there viewing images of people fucking, people sucking, people screaming in orgasmic frenzy with the same disaffected countenance that I assume when I watch Animal Planet. The porn starlets with their gigantic breasts and gaping holes, and their male counterparts with their colossal members, were nothing more than naked mammals mating on film. Porn had become background; it was little more than wallpaper to me. It took years to become excited by porn again.

We had a massive box of porn in the office that was pillaged on a daily basis by most of the employees. It was filled with low-grade, clearance porn flicks that the owner received at a discount from the various adult video stores in the neighborhood. These were the six-hour

90

porn films with a fat and sweaty Ron Jeremy in at least five scenes and titles such as *Sweet & Sour Slits*, or *Crazy Cum Fiesta*, or my personal favorite porn series, *The Blowjob Adventures of Dr. Fellatio, Volumes 1-39*. Depending on the manager on duty, we would usually watch at least three to four different films per shift. One of my managers, Pepper, was the exception. Pepper was an irascible black man in his late forties who had been working in the adult entertainment industry for over half his life. I heard that his real name was Maurice, but if you called him that, he'd slap you in the face. Pepper was the stage name he used when he danced for Chippendales in the mid-eighties, and he preferred that to his birth name. We weren't allowed to question any of Pepper's management decisions for, as he never failed to point out, he had been working in the industry longer than most of us had been alive:

"Yo! You can shut the fuck up right now cuz I seen it all, man. You ain't gonna teach Pepper shit. Bitch, go get yo fine ass up on that motherfucking stage. Damn."

I dreaded working with Pepper because he scared the shit out of me, and it was more than obvious that he didn't like me. Personally, I think he distrusted white people, but he never told me the actual reason he disliked me. He'd just say, "There are two kinds of people in this world: people you dig and people you don't. You're in the second category." Even though he had retired from stripping over a decade ago, he worked out constantly to maintain his bodybuilder physique. He combed his relaxed hair straight back and wore two or three thick gold chains over the lapels of his shimmering emerald three-piece suits. He looked like the comedian Katt Williams on steroids. Pepper ruled Foxys with the iron

91

fist of a seventies pimp. One particular area where he asserted his authority was porn film selection. Pepper only liked blowjob films, in particular, the Dr. Fellatio series. What I found remarkable about these films was that every shot consisted of a man's erect penis in the mouth of a young woman. And every scene concluded with the man climaxing in the woman's face, and that was it. There were no other sexual positions and very little female nudity. In fact, the woman's naked body was never fully displayed. It was simply one dick after another in the mouth of a different girl. I suppose if you really liked oral sex you'd find these films quite appealing, but I always found them rather boring. Pepper obviously had a fixation with oral sex, which was evident by his oft-repeated adage that "if a woman can suck the head off yo dick, then she'd make a good wife." He firmly believed that a woman who was willing to please a man orally until climax without sexual reciprocation of any kind is a woman who would dutifully tend to a man in other areas of the relationship.

"Listen here, if you have a bitch who will suck yo dick till you blow yo load and then get up and do the dishes, mop the floor, wash your motherfuckin' car, and make yo supper, you better marry that bitch. Cuz if you don't, Pepper will. And I ain't fucking around. I'll marry a bitch like that. Damn."

Pepper invariably began or ended every statement with a perfunctory "Damn." For the better part of every shift, he leaned on the DJ booth with his left arm resting on top of the CD player and, completely ignoring the girl dancing onstage, commented on the dick slurping that was occurring on the screen before us:

"Damn. Now that bitch can suck a dick. Look at that shit. That is some dick-sucking lips. You know what I'm sayin? DSLs. Are you watching, boy?" He punched me several times on the shoulder to make sure that my undivided attention was on the screen. "Damn. She loves that shit. She wants more dick. Bitch can't get enough dick. That bitch loves sucking dick. I'd bet she'd suck three dicks at one time. I'd marry that bitch. Damn. You ever have a bitch suck yo dick and yo friends' dicks? No. Hell no, you ain't never had that shit. Don't lie to me, boy. Goddamn. You white boys don't know how to get yo freak on. Get yo'self a sista and yo'll get yo freak on. Damn."

I stood there, feigned interest, and nodded in silent concurrence with everything he said. In truth, I didn't want him to punch my shoulder again. Pepper claimed to be a black belt in Tae Kwon Do, and his punches were quite painful. Not to mention, he was practically twice my size. Frequently, I'd end my shift with a massive purple bruise on my shoulder. The majority of scenes involved two white people, but there were at least one or two scenes in every Dr. Fellatio film that had either two black people or a black man and a white woman. The latter were Pepper's favorite. His eyes lit up when he saw a gigantic black penis looming in front of a nervous white woman. He punched me really hard to make sure that I was watching those scenes.

"Now that's what I'm talkin' about. Finally got a real dick up on that screen. Fourteen-inch Alabama Black Snake. Goddamn. She finna dig that shit. All bitches love the taste of black dick. They might say they don't. But that means they lying ass hoes. Cuz all bitches love the taste of black dick. Know what I'm sayin'? Heh, heh. I know you don't cuz

93

you ain't got a black dick. You white boys ain't got nothing on that shit. Damn."

Grinning with pride, he laughed loudly and repeatedly slammed my shoulder with his fist. Not knowing the proper response, I would usually smile and anxiously laugh along with him while vainly attempting to block his blows. Sometimes, I'd picture myself with a fourteen-inch black cock attached to my diminutive Semitic frame. I just don't think a huge black dick would pan out for me all that well. I'm quite certain that most girls would be frightened by the anomaly. Now, I think there is some credence to the urban myth that black men have larger penises on average than other races, but I don't think it's true in all cases. I was dubious of Pepper's penis-size claims. He boasted to every dancer that he had a massive penis, and he highly doubted that they could "handle his shit." And if they ever did "have his shit," they would summarily leave their white boyfriends. In my opinion, if a man, regardless of race, did indeed have a gigantic dick, would he always need to draw attention to it? Would he always need to constantly inform everyone he encounters that he possesses this mammoth cock?

"Damn. Now that bitch is scared. Look at that. She know she finna gag on that shit. She only got the tip in. Oh hell no. I'd be like open yo throat, bitch. It's Dr. Clifford Huxtable, and I finna check those motherfucking tonsils."

Normally, I ignored his nonsensical blathering, but on this occasion I chose to correct him. "Actually, Pepper, it was Dr. Heathcliff Huxtable, or Cliff, which was what his wife called him." He looked at me

94

incredulously for about three or four seconds before nailing my shoulder with a crushing blow.

"Shut the fuck up. I know that nigga's name. Ain't too many black doctors on the TV. Shit. This white boy thinks he knows *The Cosby Show*. Next thing you be telling me Fred Sanford worked at a motherfuckin' liberry. Damn." He returned his attention to the dick slurping on the big screen still shaking his head in disbelief. "Now that's fucked up. White bitches be scared of that black dick. They scared at first, but then they learn to love it. Yo, you got a white bitch, right?"

"Well, yeah, I guess."

"You guess. What, you can't tell the bitch is white? You never know these days with the weaves and spray tans and shit. She ever been with a nigga?" As usual, he didn't wait for my response and answered his own question, "Nah. I didn't think so. That shit ain't right. All bitches should be wit' at least one nigga. It should be a law and shit. Damn." I chose to remain silent even though I was curious as to how the state would enforce such legislation.

Pepper refused to watch any porn films other than *The Blowjob Adventures of Dr. Fellatio* series. I don't know if he even liked other porn films. He told me that he truly believed porn was degrading to women, but he fervently enjoyed watching "a bitch give head. Damn. I ain't never get sick of that shit." And, he never tired of these blowjob films. In fact, Pepper was usually too lazy to put in a new film and would just let the machine rewind the one that we had already watched and we'd be fortunate enough to watch it again. And again. And again. Most of the time we watched the same blowjob film five or six times a shift. I worked four night shifts at Foxys and only one day shift a week, and I worked with Pepper for three of those shifts over a period of six months. According to my calculations, I must have watched the movie *The Blowjob Adventures of Dr. Fellatio, Volume 33* over 500 times. Years have passed, and I still know every scene of that film. I envisage myself fifty years from now, a lecherous old goat popping Viagra while strolling into a dingy porn theater to see if I can still manage an erection. As I stumble into the dark room searching for a secluded seat, I look up and see *The Blowjob Adventures of Dr. Fellatio, Volume 33* playing on the big screen. I stand there staring blankly at the screen, and all of a sudden, I feel my entire being shudder with a tidal wave of complete and total recognition. In slow motion, I crumple to the ground knees first, and then roll onto my right side, mouth foaming, in a fit of apoplexy. My tongue darts in and out of my mouth, my hands clawing at the air. Four men dressed in white clothing place my withered old husk onto a gurney, and I'm wheeled out of the theater and into the dementia wing of some convalescent home, the whole time incoherently muttering, "Damn. That bitch can't get enough dick. She loves that shit. Goddamn."

Pepper was the only manager that forbade us to watch other porn films. Most of the other managers didn't care as long as we were watching some kind of porn film. One of my favorite managers, Patrick, used to have fun with Foxys' porn mandate. Patrick was a functioning alcoholic in his mid-thirties and one of the more sartorially challenged men I had ever met, but the reason we got along so well was that he possessed a rather odd sense of humor. It was more than obvious that the dancers despised the perpetual porn films. Not that they were feminists who were outraged by sexual exploitation; they hated the porn because it drew the customers' attention away from their stage show. They had a legitimate complaint. Customers, especially during the day shift, would sit there for hours, drinking free carbonated beverages and staring at the sex acts on the screen, wholly oblivious to the naked girl on the main stage. They wouldn't tip, buy dances, or acknowledge their presence in any way. They ignored the stage show and focused solely on the porn. This enraged the dancers. Some cursed directly at the customers from the stage while others incessantly complained to the manager or asked me to say something over the microphone. I usually obliged.

"Gentlemen, I know you didn't come all the way to the Foxys to watch porn. You can do that at home. You came here to party with real live pussy. So, fellas, let's head upstairs and buy a lap dance. Go get the real thing. Or at the very least, tip the girl onstage, you fucking perverts."

But despite my best efforts, they still didn't tip or buy private dances. The managers generally disregarded the girls' complaints and were content with the customers' apparent lack of interest in their stage shows. Pepper actually sided with the customers.

"If I walked into this motherfucker and saw yo hurt ass on stage, I'd be watchin' a skin flick my own self. Damn."

Patrick was the only manager who listened to their pleas. When they complained to him, he looked at them with an earnest expression of real concern and nodded his head empathetically. He gingerly rubbed their shoulders and replied, "Don't fret, my dears. I will wreak justice on these vile miscreants." Words like "vile" and "miscreant" were part of his typical vernacular. I think he spent his nights snorting rails of speed and reading Hawthorne novels so that he could confuse the dancers with words that they will probably never learn the meaning of nor ever hear again. Initially, they stared at him perplexedly, trying to figure out if he was serious, but in a few moments they'd pace through the club eager to find out what vengeance their fearless manager had in mind.

Patrick enjoyed ridiculing the perverts about as much as I did and brought in his own porn videos for this very purpose. He collected bizarre pornography that ran the gamut from German scat films and barnyard bestiality to Brazilian transsexual amputee films. I am not sure whether he collected these movies for shock value or sexual gratification, but he was very proud of his collection and considered pornography an unappreciated art form. It never failed to amuse me when he played a film from his private collection. These films were for extreme circumstances when it was obvious that the customers were merely taking up space and not spending any money. He never played these movies when the club was crowded or when he knew that the GM was in the vicinity. In his mind, it was better to disgust them and make them leave the club than have them waste any more of our time, but in reality, I think he relished the shock value of it all. Not only would the customers be disgusted, the dancers would be disgusted and loudly express their revulsion by laughing, screaming, and telling each other that Patrick is "a crazy motherfucker" or "one weird dude." But, they also took pleasure in watching the stingy patrons, who they previously had complained about, become uncomfortable and hastily exit the club. It was hilarious to watch them suddenly overcome with simultaneous feelings of confusion and revulsion. Allow me to create the scene:

Over the past two hours, the pervs had sat in the club swilling soda, ignoring the dancers, and staring vacantly at *Cum Fiesta* playing on the big screen. Without warning, the movie stops and the screen becomes blank. They anxiously glance around the room, trying to figure out what happened. A test screen slowly comes into focus, and they breathe a collective sigh of relief as another film begins to play. Their attention is once again diverted to the screen where an attractive exotic woman with her back to the camera is disrobing in front of a man. Then, the woman turns around, and to their utter horror, she reveals her large, uncircumcised penis. Most of them would shield their eyes and turn away disgusted and bewildered. The remainder ceased watching once they saw the man sodomizing the transsexual. I don't know if they considered it a threat to their sexuality or if they realized that we were mocking them, but you could tell they were visibly disturbed. Now, they had no choice but to pay attention to the girl onstage, buy a dance, or compromise their heterosexuality and watch the tranny porn. The Mexican customers seemed to be particularly bothered by the homosexual acts and would openly express their dissatisfaction with grunts and curses as they shuffled out of the club. A similar reaction occurred with the German scat films and the midget porn. What kept me entertained was that Patrick would continue to play the movie even after the customers had left. The girls begged and pleaded with him to turn it off, but he would laugh, shake his head, and tell them that they got what they asked for. And they did. They released the Kraken and now had to deal with it. I loved working at Foxys for this reason. Since I no longer found porn sexually arousing, I was pleased that there still existed some type of porn that I at least found entertaining.

Doug the Retard

"Hey, can you piss for me?"

"Right now? I just went to the bathroom ten minutes ago," I replied, sounding a bit annoyed with the question.

"Fuck. I guess I can wait. Do you have a cigarette?" Zoe asked as she jumped onto the stool next to the soundboard. Zoe was a diminutive brunette who barely stood five feet tall even wearing her stilettos. Though she was around twenty-five, she looked like a twelve-year-old wearing a neon green g-string. I felt like I was committing a crime by lighting her cigarette. Her beauty was disarming, and her youthful appearance made her quite popular amongst the true sexual deviants and fetishists who frequented the Ruby Club. Zoe had a host of perverted regulars who visited her on different days of the week. At least three times during her shift, she'd escape to the DJ booth for a cigarette break and to complain about the requests that she received from them. We became good friends, and I'd always try to lend a sympathetic ear to her travails and help her out whenever I could. This afternoon, she had one of her more insufferable regulars, Chad the Piss Guy, waiting for her to return with a champagne glass filled with her urine.

"Look, I'll give you twenty dollars if you piss for me. Please."

"Zoe, it skeeves me out knowing that a man is drinking my urine. I'm sorry."

"I think it's fucking funny," she said, giggling. "I just had to sit there for two hours and listen to Chad tell me how his wife makes him wear a strap-on and fuck her because he can't keep his dick hard."

"Damn, no wonder that guy is so fucked up."

"He kept making me call him an impotent piece of shit and slap him in the face."

"I'm sure you enjoyed that."

"I did, actually. Check out what he bought me." She reached into her purse and pulled out two tampons. "Other girls get jewelry. I get fucking tampons."

"Well, it's a very utilitarian gift."

"Yeah, just what I needed. Tampons. He said he wants me to use them next time I'm having my period and save them for him. He said he'd pay me $200 per used tampon."

"That's not bad. And what does he plan to do with them?"

"He said he wants me to slap him in the face with it and then jam it in his mouth." Zoe frowned and shook her head as she crushed her cigarette in the ashtray.

"That guy is a freak of nature. I can't believe he's married."

"And he has two teenage kids." She held up the empty champagne glass and pointed it at me. "So, are you going to piss for me or what?"

"As long as you hold the glass for me."

"Fine," she said with a shrug. I locked the door to the DJ booth, unzipped my pants, and shoved the head of my cock in the glass. Within twenty seconds, it was filled with warm yellow urine. "You need to drink more water." Zoe smiled and held the piss-filled glass up in the air. "To health and happiness!" she chimed and handed me a crumpled twenty-dollar bill. "And thank you for your services. Now, to watch Chad sip on your piss while I tell him how much of a limp dick piece of shit he is."

"Anytime, darling." I unlocked the door and held it open as Zoe sauntered by carefully gripping the champagne glass to prevent any spillage.

When discussing strip club patrons, it's essential to distinguish between normal customers and regular customers. The former typically visit strip clubs in groups and usually for an event such as a bachelor party, birthday, or company outing. They range from frat boys and military men to businessmen showing their visiting clients a good time. Their motivation is to have a good night out on the town, tip the girls onstage, get a few lap dances, have a few drinks, and then leave. They do not visit a strip club to engender a personal relationship with the girls who work there. And that is the principal difference between normal customers and regular customers. Regulars frequent a strip club several times a week and almost always by themselves. They schedule their visits in advance with the dancer and usually show up at the same time each week. I'd recognize a lot of regulars during day shifts because the club was less crowded and it was easier for the dancers to spend more time with them. At the Ruby, the dancers would spend at least three hours with their regular customers, and the visit would encompass a meal and VIP-area lap dances. Not only would they make $1,000 from the visit, they often received expensive gifts, such as jewelry, lingerie, and cellphones. Depending on the duration and intensity of the relationship, some regulars went so far as pay a dancer's monthly rent, buy them new cars, and finance their breast implants and other forms of cosmetic surgery. But despite all the gifts and money, their relationship with the dancer rarely developed into one of a sexual nature. What they have is a sexless relationship based solely on commodity, which is exactly what most regulars desire. A lot of these men are married with families, and the fantasy of an extramarital affair is more exciting and convenient than actually having one. This way they have a faux relationship with a beautiful woman who would never look at them twice outside the club. If sexual gratification was their goal, they could easily afford to purchase an escort for the night; but what motivates the regular is the interactive fantasy of this faux relationship. They willingly suspend their disbelief, and for a few hours each week, they have the undivided attention of a beautiful, exotic dancer who acts like she's sexually interested and enjoys spending time with them. This type of regular tends to be an older gentleman who might have a dying spouse or is recently widowed, and the dancer he visits reminds him of his youth or provides him with an opportunity to escape from his problems. I've heard more than one dancer comment that it's extremely creepy when their regular shows them a picture of his deceased wife in her early twenties and then tells the poor girl how much she resembles the dead woman. I worked with one girl who had a regular that would bring his deceased wife's bathing suits and beg her to model them. Initially, she flat out refused, but eventually he offered her enough money that she complied regardless of how disquieting the experience.

But there are several other less innocuous types of regulars who frequent strip clubs. I've always been fond of the fetishists. Chad the Piss Guy fit perfectly within this category. It would be difficult for Chad to walk into a normal bar and find a girl who would be willing to sit with him for several hours while he complained about his impotence and begged her to let him drink her urine. Whereas, at the strip club, as long as there's money involved, there's no judgment. For $500, almost any girl I worked with would scream invectives at Chad while he drank their urine. There were quite a few dancers who worked as professional dominatrixes, and they preferred the fetishist regulars. I knew a 6'2" Amazonian dancer named Blondie who operated her own dungeon in South San Francisco but still worked at the clubs to earn extra money. She had a regular who would visit her once a week who enjoyed having her shove her used panties in his mouth while kneeing him in the testicles as hard as she could. Blondie confessed that she found his visits to be cathartic, but I never asked her to explain. I learned from experience that it's best to avoid asking the reason these girls work in the industry. But regardless of the amount of compensation, it takes a thick skin and a high measure of tolerance to deal with the fetishists. I once worked with a seasoned stripper and prostitute named Violet who had been working at brothels and strip clubs across the country since she was in her late teens. She was in her early thirties when I worked with her at the Doll House, and looking at her face in daylight, it was obvious that her lifestyle had taken its toll on her appearance. Violet had some incredible, cringe-inducing stories, and she rarely seemed unhinged by any of the odd characters she serviced, with the exception of one type of fetish. Keep in mind, I never inquired the reason why this particular fetish bothered her while the ones that sounded much worse were tolerable. I probably didn't want to know the answer.

"Jesus, that was the longest 2-for-1 I've ever done." Violet sighed heavily as she walked into the DJ booth. Her hands fumbled with the clasps of her bikini top, and I noticed that she hadn't bothered to put on her bottoms yet. Though I tried not to stare, Violet had the strangest-shaped labia I had ever seen. They dangled like burgundy caterpillars on either side of her vagina. I assumed that that was the result of many years in her profession.

"The two songs were three minutes a piece, like all the rest of the specials."

"I know. It just seemed like it was never gonna end. I have an annoying regular here today. He's sitting over there waiting for you to run another 2-for-1." She pointed to a thin, balding middle-aged white guy tapping his fingers nervously on the table while staring disinterestedly at the porn film playing on the movie screen.

"What? Is he cheap?"

"No. He's a fucking freak. He comes here once a week with his speculum and penlight. And I have to stand over him while he shoves his fucking speculum in my pussy and shines the light up there," she remarked with disgust.

"That's kinda gross. Do you ask him to give you a pap smear at least?"

"Shut the fuck up. He's a freak. Today he brought Star Wars figures. I told him he had to put a condom on before he put them in. And he was upset about that. But you have to draw a line with these guys. If he didn't pay me good money, I'd tell him to fuck off." I wondered what "good money" meant to Violet. I didn't ask, but I doubt that guy was paying her more than sixty dollars per 2-for-1 special.

"Which Star Wars figures: Chewbacca or Darth Vader?"

"I don't fucking know. I let him put the gold guy and a stormtrooper in there." I imagined Violet could literally fit the Millennium Falcon inside her vagina.

"Well, it's good of you to indulge his fantasies."

"Whatever. I always get the fucking speculum guys. I'll be back. I'm gonna smoke."

While the fetishists were the most interesting regulars, there were a couple other types who were also amusing. I never tired of the "Captain Save-A-Ho" regular. These regulars were typically older men who made it their mission to persuade the dancer to leave the industry and live a more virtuous life. They would visit at least once a week and offer to pay for their college tuition or rehab, or help them find other means of employment. Oftentimes, they would pay for their child's medical treatments and help with living expenses. These regulars attempted to create a seemingly wholesome father-daughter relationship with the dancer, but there was invariably an underlying element of perversion. A lot of the strippers preferred this type of regular because they usually didn't have to give them private dances. The captains portrayed themselves as these platonic friends who just wanted to have a conversation and compensate them for their time. In my opinion, the Captain Save-A-Ho regular was a first cousin to the Megalomaniac regular. While the Megalomaniac used his money to exert his power over the dancers, the Captain Save-A-Ho did the exact same thing but under a veneer of altruism. Typically, the Megalomaniacs were much wealthier than the Captain Save-A-Hos, and sometimes they would buy two or three dancers at a time and have them perform private lesbian shows and group lap dances. These men had disposable incomes, and their fantasy was to see what they could force a beautiful woman to do for money. They would ply the girls with ecstasy, cocaine, and expensive champagne, but their primary intent was domination and ultimately humiliation. It was a power game for them, and their money allowed them to control these women. A lot of these guys were unattractive, obscenely wealthy men who were aroused by humiliating young beautiful women. They were well aware that these women despised them but needed their money, and that was the essential component of the fantasy. You could argue that the Megalomaniacs were fetishists, but instead of being kicked in the testicles, their fetish was dominance.

Poor Zoe had one of the most notorious Megalomaniac regulars at the Ruby Club. What made him even more difficult to deal with was that he was severely handicapped. The dancers called him Doug the Retard even though he wasn't actually retarded. Doug reminded me of a slightly younger Larry Flynt. He was in his early fifties and had similar fleshy jowls, thinning reddish hair, and a petulant disposition. He was also a wheelchair-bound paraplegic, which is the main reason I thought he looked like the infamous publisher. Doug had been frequenting the Ruby Club for years, and every dancer who had worked there for more than six months had the unfortunate experience of spending at least one afternoon with him. He would buy one or two girls for a four-hour ordeal, which involved multiple full-contact lap dances, degrading demands, unpleasant odors, and the worst part: a meal that they had to feed to him. It was an arduous experience for even the seasoned strippers, and though he paid them quite well for their time, most did not want to endure him more than once. There were only a couple girls who counted Doug as a regular, and Zoe was one of them. I knew when Doug had shown up at the club because the dancers would hide away in the DJ booth until his handler had procured his luckless prey for him.

"Oh my god. I can't fucking deal with him today," cried Zoe in exasperation as she threw open the door of the booth, snatched my cigarettes off the counter, and shoved one between her thin red lips. "It's too fucking much. I can't deal."

"Doug?" I asked, knowing full well whom she was referring to.

"Yeah," she replied, deeply inhaling and suddenly noticing that there was another dancer in the room sitting on a chair with her legs tightly crossed, her attention fixated on her cellphone screen. The slender, blonde dancer was named Haley, and she had been texting for the past half hour. In fact, I had forgotten that she was still there.

"He's not easy to deal with. I feel for you." I reached over and gave her shoulders a brief sympathy massage before checking the CD player to see how much time I had left of the current song.

"I was giving him a lap dance and trying to pull his hands out of my g-string when he smacked my ass and called me an ungrateful whore."

"What'd you do?"

"I slapped him in the face, and then he started laughing and asked me to do it again. So I hit him three more times as hard as I could."

"Jesus. What'd he do?"

"He fucking shit his pants and kept screaming, "Uh oh. Poopie pants. Uh oh, poopie pants."

"That's fucking gross."

"You have no idea. I could feel him shit on my thighs, and the smell. Fuck. It smelled so bad. I almost puked all over him."

"He probably would've loved that."

"I'm sure he would. Sick fuck," Zoe hissed as she smashed her cigarette into the ashtray.

"You know he stinks and he's crippled, but he's got money, girl," said a nasally voice. We both looked over and saw that Haley had put her cellphone down and, uninvited, entered our conversation. "Last time I danced for him he gave me $1,000."

"Yeah, but did he shit while you were giving him a dance?"

"Girl, as long as it doesn't touch me. He can shit his pants all fucking night. I just want his money."

"Then why doesn't he take you?"

"Because he doesn't want me. He knows I just want his money. He wants you because you're affected." She walked over and gently brushed a lock of Zoe's hair away from her face. "Look at you, darlin', you're holding back tears."

"No, I'm not," Zoe choked. Her eyes were quivering.

"It's okay. You can cry back here. I have many times. Just wipe away those tears when you go back to him. Don't let that bastard see you cry." Tears streamed down Zoe's tiny cheeks, and Haley knelt down and wiped them off with a tissue. "It's okay, darlin'."

Feeling a bit awkward, I diverted my attention to picking out the next song for the dancer on stage. When I turned back around, both girls had left the booth. Though Zoe had to experience a horrendous ordeal, it sounded like she would be more than adequately compensated. Two hours later, she returned to the booth in a much better mood and wearing her street clothes, which consisted of dark jeans and a hoodie.

"Hey, are you splitting? I take it Doug has left the building."

"I don't know and I don't care. He paid me $1,500, so I'm getting the fuck out of here. Here you go, honey." She handed me a $100 bill. "Thanks for dealing with me today."

"Thanks, Zoe. You know I'm always here when you need me."

Zoe stood on the tips of her toes and gave me a hug and a kiss. "Thanks, Dave. You have a good night."

"You have a good night, too." She flashed a quick smile and disappeared down the hall.

I still had three hours left of an uneventful Friday day shift. I noticed that Trinity was coming up next, and since I knew she loved eighties music, I grabbed an eighties compilation and selected the fifth track, Hall and Oates's "I Can't Go For That." I had to piss, but I had to start Trinity's song and introduce her before leaving the booth. I cut the current dancer's song short, introduced Trinity, and flipped on the compilation. By this point, my bladder felt like it was about to burst. I bolted to the upstairs bathroom at the end of the hall, but the door was locked. Fuck. I had to use the downstairs bathroom. I ran through the VIP area and bounded down the stairs to the first floor. Most restrooms at strip clubs are deplorable, and the one at Ruby was no exception. It reeked of semen, shit, cigarette smoke, and Lysol disinfectant. Luckily, the bathroom was empty and I slid into the first stall and relieved myself. That piss felt better than my last six orgasms combined. In fact, it felt so good that I needed a smoke afterwards. Since there was no one around, I figured I'd sneak a bump or two and help the remainder of my shift go by a bit quicker. I dipped the tip of a key into the baggie and snorted several shards of crystal into my right nostril. It burned as it entered my nasal passage, causing me to gag reflexively. I was about to do another bump when I heard a moaning sound. I ignored it—after working at a few clubs, I had learned that it's best to pretend not to hear or see most things—and held the key up to my nostril, when I heard the sound again. This time it was louder and protracted. It sounded as if someone was in a lot of pain. I hastily snorted the bump and shoved the keys and the baggie back into my pocket. Stepping out of the stall, I looked around to see if anyone else had entered the bathroom. No one else was there. I heard another moan. It seemed to be coming from the handicapped stall at the end. Hesitantly, I approached the stall and leaned into the door to push it open, but something was obstructing it. It wasn't locked and I could push it open an inch or two, but there was definitely something solid blocking the door. Finally, I gave the door a hard shove and heard an anguished groan come from inside the stall. Peering in, I could see a man lying in a crumpled heap on the floor, his arm extended weakly upwards in a futile effort to grab the metal railing. A foul stench emanated from the stall, and there was a brownish liquid seeping out of the man's right side. He noticed me staring at him and meekly whispered for help. I sidestepped out of the stall's doorway to contemplate this situation. I didn't need this right now. I really didn't have time to deal with a drunken idiot. I leaned my head back in the doorway to take another look and suddenly realized the identity of the man lying on the floor in his own excrement. It was Doug the Retard.

"Hey. I need some help. Can you help me?" Doug had a very low, guttural voice that was difficult to understand. It was practically a croak.

I didn't respond. Instead, I quickly exited the lavatory and went to find someone else to help him. Luckily, I ran into Big Jeff, one of the club's enormous bouncers, coming into the bathroom.

"Jeff, dude, we have a situation here. You're going to have to deal with it because I gotta head upstairs."

"A situation?"

"Yeah, check it out."

We walked to the third stall. Jeff opened the door and started laughing till he had to wipe tears from his eyes.

"That motherfucker is lying in a pile of shit. Fuckin' mudslide." Still laughing, he then walked over to the urinal and relieved himself.

"Do you know where his caregiver guy is? Someone needs to help him out."

"Caregiver? What the fuck's a caregiver? You're on your own with this one, buddy. I don't clean up shit."

"His nurse. Can you find the guy who takes care of him? We gotta help him out."

"All right, calm the fuck down. I'll help you." Jeff walked into the first stall, grabbed a roll of toilet paper, and tossed it to me. "Here you go, man. Knock yourself out."

He left the bathroom laughing loudly. In a panic, I ran outside to look for Doug's caregiver, but he was nowhere to be found. It was possible that Doug had come by himself but highly unlikely. I returned to the foul-smelling bathroom and walked over to the ailing man.

"Hey, where's your nurse?"

He tried to lift himself up to look at me, but his hand slipped in the shit puddle and he slammed back onto the ground. "I fired that fucking prick. Fuck him. Now give me a hand," he slurred angrily.

Doug was inebriated, and apparently he had fallen and shit himself while lying on the bathroom floor. Not knowing how to handle this situation, I watched him try to lift himself up again, this time using his collapsed wheelchair for support. I cautiously approached him and extended my hand, careful to watch my step. The stench was overbearing, and I held my breath while I struggled to pull him off the ground. He was almost to his feet when he slipped in the shit puddle and practically pulled me on top of him. I narrowly avoided stepping in it, and forced my legs out to maintain balance. Doug crashed to the floor and lay there groaning for a few moments, trying to catch his breath. Once again, I grasped his left hand and attempted to pull him upright.

This time he pushed off the toilet with his right hand and managed to stand shakily on his withered, malformed legs. I leaned him against the wall and picked up his wheelchair, unfolded it, and rolled it to him. He muttered something that sounded like either "asshole" or "bless your soul" and wheeled himself to the sink.

"Hey, are you okay? I gotta go upstairs and change the song."

"I'm fine. Thank you," he growled in his raspy voice.

Having no idea how to extricate myself from this awkward scene, I just turned around and briskly walked out of the bathroom. I thought it was best if both of us forgot that this encounter ever occurred. I didn't know if he had another nurse he could call to drive him home, but I didn't wait around to find out. The following week, I was working my Friday day shift when a well-groomed man who resembled John Waters in a white nurse's uniform walked into the booth and timidly asked, "Excuse me, are you the DJ who helped Doug out last week?"

"Doug the Re—" I almost said "retard" but luckily caught myself. "Umm, Yeah. Why?"

"Doug's very grateful that you helped him and would like to buy you dinner tomorrow."

I was taken aback and didn't quite know how to respond. "It's okay. He doesn't have to do that." Honestly, I could think of many other things I'd rather do than have dinner with Doug the Retard, such as going to the dentist or renewing my driver's license at the DMV.

"Oh, but he insists and, trust me, Doug's not fond of rejection," he said indifferently.

"Well, okay, but I have plans tomorrow, so I can't have dinner with him."

"How about Sunday evening?"

114

"I have something going on Sunday too. I'm booked this weekend. Sorry."

"Listen, Doug will keep sending me back here to invite you to dinner. He will not accept 'no' as an answer. Please have dinner with him, and we both can move on with our lives."

I took a couple moments to survey the serious expression on the nurse's face and realized that this was far from a joke. "Okay. I'm not working Monday."

"Excellent. I will make reservations at Gary Danko at 6:00 PM."

"Gary Danko?" I had never eaten there but knew it was one of the most expensive restaurants in the city.

"Yes, that's Doug's favorite restaurant. Please don't be late. Doug is not fond of tardiness."

I couldn't care less what Doug was fond of, but this dinner sounded like it might not be so bad after all. Gary Danko is one of the finest dining establishments in the city, and I'd heard it takes three months to get a reservation there for a regular person. I was sure Doug spent so much money there that they treated him like royalty. Regardless, it had been a long time since I had lobster, and this would be one of those rare occasions that I could order the highest-priced items on the menu and not feel the least bit of remorse.

That Monday evening, trying my best to be punctual, I left my apartment at quarter to six and caught a cab heading up Polk Street. The cab driver looked at me twice when I told him my destination and asked, "You going to work?"

"No, I'm having dinner there," I replied, not trying to conceal my annoyance. I'm sure I didn't look like the typical Gary Danko habitué, but I was wearing a Calvin Klein black dress shirt tucked into a creased pair of black slacks. I even wore a tie for the occasion. Whatever. This might be the only opportunity for me to eat at Gary Danko, and I was not about to let a surly cab driver ruin my mood. "The reservation's at six, so I'd appreciate it if you could step on it."

Though I couldn't tell for sure, it looked like the driver rolled his eyes when I said that and he continued driving at the exact same pace. It rarely does any good to tell an urban cab driver to "step on it." The restaurant is located in the Fisherman's Wharf neighborhood, which was about fifteen minutes from my apartment, and since there was little traffic, we arrived shortly before six. A doorman opened the door of the cab and escorted me into the dimly lit restaurant. I noticed immediately that the décor was a bit more modern than I had expected and had a very Upper East Side Manhattan vibe to it. As soon as I walked in, a blonde hostess with an unflattering toothy smile cheerfully piped, "Welcome to Gary Danko. Do you have a reservation tonight?"

"I'm here to meet Doug," I said shakily, suddenly realizing that I didn't even know Doug's surname.

"Oh, okay. Hold on a moment." She whispered something to an attractive woman with short brown hair standing to her right and then shifted her attention back to me. "Autumn will show you to Doug's table."

Doug obviously was a regular here if the staff knew him by his first name, though I doubted there were many disgruntled paraplegics who frequented this restaurant. I followed Autumn down a dark hallway to the second dining room. She led me to a cozy banquette in the corner, and I slid into the cushioned booth opposite Doug who was seated in his wheelchair. For being such an ogre, he almost looked handsome in his black suit and dark blue tie. He watched me closely as I sat down, and waited till I composed myself before saying anything.

"Thanks for coming. I appreciate what you did for me the other day," he growled.

"Thanks for inviting me. I don't think I ever formally introduced myself. My name is Da—"

"I know your name," Doug said curtly, cutting me off. "Would you like some champagne?"

"Okay." I reached over and picked up a bottle of Dom Pérignon from the bucket and poured myself a tall glass. I noticed that Doug had a massive mound of caviar on a platter in front of him.

"Are we out of champagne? I'll ask the dickheads to bring another bottle. Do you like fish shit?" he asked, shoving the platter of caviar over to me.

"Thanks," I said as I picked up a spoon and deposited a generous glob of caviar on a cracker. Doug was still staring at me with an intensity that made me feel uncomfortable. "So, do you dine here often?"

"I know the owner. That's the reason these dickheads have to kiss my crippled ass. Watch this. Hey, shithead. Yeah, I'm talking to you. Why don't you bring me another bottle?" he shouted, holding up the half-empty bottle of Dom. He then slammed it down on the table. "These fucking pricks don't know hospitality from their assholes."

The server that he screamed at hurriedly ran off to fetch another bottle of the $300 champagne. I focused my attention on the menu, thinking that the sooner I ordered my entrée the sooner I'd be able to leave. It didn't come as much of a surprise that Doug wasn't the most agreeable dining companion. The server returned with the new bottle and apprehensively placed it in the bucket next to the half-empty bottle, eyeing Doug the entire time and preparing for a sharp rebuke. But Doug ignored him. His attention was also focused on his menu.

"I take it you've never been here before."

"Umm, no I haven't," I responded, not knowing whether he was being condescending.

"Well, it's a five-course dinner. Feel free to order anything you want. I don't fucking care."

"Okay. Thanks." I doled out another generous portion of caviar on a cracker and was about to take a bite when our server approached the table. He was a young man in his mid-twenties, and, judging by his steeled countenance, I could tell that he had served Doug in the past.

"Hello, gentlemen. Have you made your selection?" he said with a slight lisp, looking at Doug.

"Why don't you ask my friend over there. I'm still deciding."

"All right. Sir, have you made your selection?"

I could tell that he was a bit surprised that Doug referred to anyone as a friend, let alone someone my age. "Umm, I will have the oysters and asparagus salad to start with and the Maine Lobster as the entree."

"Excellent choice, sir. Doug, have you made up your mind?"

"I'll have some oysters, the risotto, and the beef filet. You know how I like it."

"I most certainly do. Gentlemen, I'll return with some sparkling water in a minute," he said, and then disappeared into the dining room.

"You know these restaurants only hire faggots?" Doug had resumed staring at me with the same uncomfortable intensity as before.

"Well, there are a lot of gay people in this town, and they need jobs too."

"Really, I had no fucking clue," he croaked sarcastically. "What did you think of my new nurse?

"He seemed very friendly."

Doug roared with laughter that rapidly devolved into a fit of coughs, sputters, and chokes. "Friendly," he said, barely being able to spit out the word. His face was red, and he took a moment to regain composure before continuing, "He's a faggot too. I told him that if he gets an erection when he wipes my ass, he's fired." He burst into another laugh-coughing fit that lasted for several minutes. He finally stopped when he realized I wasn't laughing at all. "Would you lighten the fuck up? I'm just joking. Why does everyone have to be so fucking PC in this city? Here, take this." He reached into his jacket pocket, pulled out a large bag of what looked like cocaine, and flung it at me. I caught it before it would have hit me in the face, and swiftly hid it in my lap under the table, looking around anxiously to make sure none of the other diners had seen him throw it at me. The restaurant was dark, and we were seated far enough away from the other diners that I didn't think anyone noticed. But, still, I was startled.

"Jesus Fucking Christ. What the hell are you doing?"

"What do you mean? I'm giving you some blow to lighten your goddamn mood. You're too serious."

"This looks like an ounce. That's a lot of blow to be carrying around."

"I don't give a fuck. Now do it up, son."

"Here? At the table?"

"For fuck's sake," he sighed. "Give it to me."

I gently handed him the hefty sack of blow underneath the table. He snatched it from my hand and dropped the sack on the table in front of him. Pushing back the tablecloth, he then proceeded to dump out about half of the bag's contents. I was in shock and couldn't believe he was being so brazen. "Umm, what the fuck are you doing? Shouldn't we be discreet about this? That's a large quantity of cocaine you got there."

Doug glanced at me for a moment, shook his head, and started crushing rocks of cocaine with the bottom of his champagne glass. He then picked up his knife, flipped it upside down, and cut out six four-inch lines.

"Now shut the fuck up and do some blow."

He handed me a rolled up $100 bill which I used to quickly snort my two lines. The coke was harsh, and I leaned back into the booth as I felt my upper jaw and right side of my face become instantly numb. Doug snorted, grabbed the bill from me, and proceeded to inhale the four remaining lines.

"That's about as pure as you can get," he chimed as he looked over at me, noticing the overwhelmed expression on my face. Using his right hand, he clumsily scooped the rest of the pile back into the bag and returned it to his inside jacket pocket. "Feeling better now?"

I nodded. I had never done cocaine that pure, and I could feel an adrenaline rush pulsating through my entire body. I took several deep breaths to steady myself before downing my glass of champage. At this point, our server arrived with the first course. He gingerly set the asparagus salad and oysters in front of me and another plate of oysters and the risotto in front of Doug. He asked if we wanted any more champagne, and Doug ordered another bottle without bothering to look up at him. The food looked delicious but my appetite had completely vanished. I looked over at Doug and realized that he had been staring at me fixatedly for the past several minutes. Perhaps the drugs were making me paranoid. I decided to divert my attention and try one of the oysters. Thankfully, they were medium-sized, because swallowing large raw oysters is like throwing back a shot glass full of cold semen. With a small spoonful of vinagrette, I knocked back the first oyster and reached for another before noticing that Doug was still staring at me. I tried to ignore his glower by looking at the other diners in the room, but eventually it became so uncomfortable that I had to address him directly. "Did I piss you off or something? Why do you keep staring at me like that? It's rude."

As soon as I spoke up, Doug looked down at the table and then up at the ceiling and then back down at the table. "No, I'm not angry. I'm confused," he said in his croaky voice.

"About what?" At this point, I didn't really care about upsetting him. This meal was difficult to deal with, so if it ended now, I could live with that. Fuck the lobster. The cocaine had killed my appetite.

"About the reason I'm envious of you."

"Envious of me?"

"Yes, and it bothers me."

"Why would you be envious of me? You hardly know me."

"I know what you are, and I know what you do. And I'm envious of that."

"What do you mean?"

"How many of those girls do you fuck a night?"

"Well, even though it's not really any of your business, it's much less than you'd think," I answered honestly.

"Yeah, well, it's still more than me," he growled as he stared down at the table and began fidgeting with his fork. He paused for a few moments before lifting his head up and pointing the fork at me. "Here I am worth exponentially more than you and I can't even fuck one of those whores. And you, a drug-using hippie, have your pick of the litter. God is one merciless cunt."

"Fuck you, I'm not a hippie."

"Fuck me, huh? Fuck me. Do you know what I have to do to get an erection? Do you have any idea?"

"Doug, I really don't want to know. And if you're going to carry on like this, I'm leaving."

"Don't go. I apologize. My caustic nature often rubs people the wrong way."

"Really, you don't say," I remarked glibly. But I could tell by his pained expression that an apology from Doug was a rare occurrence, and I couldn't help but wonder why he extended me the courtesy.

"It's just that I don't have many friends, and I don't know how to relate to others. You would never understand how it feels to live in this useless shell of a body. I can't even manage my own continence."

Well, this dinner conversation had taken a strange twist largely due to the cocaine freeing Doug's tongue. I briefly considered steering it back to more banal topics, such as the weather or some new TV series, when I decided to seize the opportunity to ask, "What the fuck happened to you? Were you born like that?"

Doug's beady eyes squinted behind his thick glasses, and he seemed slightly startled by my question. He ruminated a few seconds before eventually responding, "I was a young, stupid prick who never appreciated what life had given me. I come from an incredibly wealthy family and have always had a silver spoon up my ass. From boarding school to university to employment at my father's company, everything has been handed to me. I never once studied for an exam in college. I didn't have to. My father's generous donations bought me a place on the honor roll. I rarely showed up for work, yet I still received a seven-figure paycheck. And the women. Oh, do I miss the fucking women." Doug raised both hands in the air as he said this as if in gratitude to some long-forgotten sex deity. "I banged supermodels, porn stars, actresses, golddiggers. You name it, I fucked it. I hosted some of the craziest swinger parties in Northern California. Believe me, nothing makes a girl hornier than cocaine and ludes. God, I wish I could relive the fucking seventies." He paused for a moment to reminisce before placing his right palm on his forehead and continuing morosely, "Then it all came to a crashing halt. Literally. It was the summer of '81, maybe '82—I forget. I went to a raging party at some mansion in Malibu. We had been partying for four days straight. By the third day, I was so intoxicated that I couldn't remember my own fucking name, and by the fourth day, I thought it was time for me to go home. This is all hearsay because I don't remember any of it, but I left the party in some guy's Porsche and sped up the Pacific Coast Highway till I ran into a utility pole, going about ninety. The car was practically torn in half. I woke up about two months later in a hospital unable to feel the lower half of my body. Doctors said it was a miracle that I survived. A miracle for them, perhaps. For me, a constant reminder of what I'll never be able to do again." Doug stopped talking and for the next minute or two sat in silence, staring at the plate of oysters in front of him, his face a rictus of deep and devastating sorrow.

I wanted to offer some words of sympathy or maybe reach over and gently pat his slumped shoulder, but really I didn't want to touch him, and I couldn't think of anything to say other than, "You got any more blow?"

123

All at once, Doug snapped out of his dark reverie and looked at me with an incredulous expression as if he couldn't believe what he had just heard. I thought he might try to stab me with the fork he was previously using as a pointer. "Fuck it!" he exclaimed triumphantly and reached into his pocket, pulled out the sack of blow, and tossed it on the table. He then snatched the bottle of Dom from the ice bucket, shoved it in his mouth, and downed it, rivulets of expensive champagne trickling down his fleshy jowls. He slammed the bottle on the table, wiped his sleeve across his chin, and once more yelled, "Fuck it!" before dumping a healthy amount of coke onto a plate and furiously cutting four massive rails. With the same rolled up $100 bill, he snorted two lines before shoving the plate over to me. "Let's do some blow and get the fuck out of here."

I snorted the two remaining lines and looked up to see our server standing next to Doug with our second course in his hands. I could tell that he had noticed the mound of cocaine on the plate in front of me, but he did his best to seem oblivious. His apparent look of displeasure reminded me of the strippers who had dealt with Doug many times before.

"Gentlemen, you seem to have lost your appetites," he said, grinning sarcastically while surveying the plates of untouched food on the table. "Are you ready for the next course, or are you still working on the first?"

"There won't be a next course. We have to leave. Charge the bill to my tab and give yourself a $500 tip," croaked Doug as he fumbled in his jacket pocket and pulled out his cellphone.

I was nonplussed. I wanted at least one bite of the lobster. This was probably the only time I'd ever dine at Gary Danko, and I didn't even eat anything. But it was too late. The server nodded and walked away carrying our dishes back to the kitchen. "So, where are we going?" I asked.

Doug ignored me and barked into his phone, "Hey, what the fuck are you doing? Pull the car around. We're going to the Paradise Club." He looked agitated as he shoved his phone into his jacket pocket. "That faggot was probably jacking off to gay porn. Not on my dime." He angrily shifted his electric wheelchair into reverse, backed up about three feet, and sped down the corridor toward the foyer of the restaurant. I was still seated when he suddenly took off, and I had to run to catch up with him. The blonde hostess with the gummy smile waved a half-hearted goodbye, obviously relieved that Doug was leaving the premises.

As soon as we walked outside, Doug's nurse drove up in a black Mercedes Benz van. He hastily exited the van, walked around to the right side, and slid open the door to reveal a folded, upright black metallic wheelchair lift. I noticed he was the same nurse who looked like John Waters, and waved "hello," but he ignored me or at least pretended not to notice the gesture. The van was missing the front passenger seat and one of the bench seats in the cabin, leaving a large open area for Doug's wheelchair. The nurse pressed a button on a remote control that lowered the hydraulic lift, and waited for Doug to safely maneuver his chair on top of it before elevating him into the vehicle. I climbed in behind Doug and sat on a black leather bucket seat in the back. The cabin area of the van was surprisingly spacious, and the walls were covered in soft black leather and adorned with a dark mahogany trim. It was definitely the most luxurious handicapped-accessible vehicle I had ever been in, but truth be told, I hadn't been in many. There was a full bar and small refrigerator where the passenger seat should have been, and a large flat-screen television hung above the driver's seat. The nurse locked Doug's wheelchair into position and handed him the remote control. Doug lifted his chubby arm towards the screen, turned on the television, and flipped through the channels before stopping at a movie.

"You know this one?"

It took me a minute to realize that we were watching the eighties movie *Porky's*. "Yeah, isn't this *Porky's*? It's been a long time since I've seen it."

"I love this fucking movie. I can watch it repeatedly and still be amused. It's the subtleties that people tend to gloss over," he said, smiling up at the screen for few seconds before shifting his attention to the nurse and frowning. "Hey, faggot, get me and my friend here a fucking drink."

Doug's nurse sighed audibly and turned around in the driver's seat. "What would you like to drink?"

I was about to mention to Doug that the reason he might have difficulty with relationships is that he acts like an asshole to everyone, but I really wanted to do some more of his drugs, so I decided to hold my tongue until I was about to leave. I did make a mental note, however, to tell Doug to stop being such a supreme prick. "I'll have some whiskey, please."

"Whiskey, good choice, sir," Doug said gleefully. He seemed giddy, like a little kid at an arcade with a pocketful of quarters. "Faggot, pour us some Balvenie."

The nurse rolled his eyes and removed two tumblers from the bar. I imagined he must be well compensated because I couldn't believe any self-respecting individual would put up with this abuse on a daily basis. He filled the tumblers with the high-end Scotch, handed one to Doug, and then walked over and handed the other glass to me. Before he returned to the driver's seat, he asked dryly, "Will that be all?"

"Yes, now take us to Paradise." Doug's nurse started up the car, and we headed southbound towards Polk Street. "'I got some tickets for paradise. Pack those bags and let's leave tonight.' Isn't that how the 'Paradise' song goes?"

"Well, actually, the song's called 'Two Tickets to Paradise,' but I understand your reference."

"Yes, I'm sure you're quite familiar with the works of Eddie Money and his contemporaries. I hear that music every time I walk into your den of iniquity."

"Who doesn't like classic rock?" I asked rhetorically, thinking about how I'd never spin that song unless a dancer refused to tip me.

"Well, it's certainly better than that nigger shit. How 'bout a toast?" Doug raised his glass high up in the air. "Here's to those who sit when they pee. We love 'em in leather. We love 'em in lace. But we love 'em the best when they sit on our face!" He laughed out loud, knocked his glass against mine, and took a large swig. "Good stuff, eh?"

"Damn fine whiskey."

"Have you ever been to Paradise Club?"

"No, I haven't, but I imagine it's a bit early to go to a dance club," I replied, looking at the clock on the van's dashboard and noticing that it was only 8:15 PM.

"I'm sure you can dance if you want to, but I like to do more than dancing, if you know what I mean." Doug laughed a creepy, guttural laugh before lifting his drink to his mouth. He set his glass down on the wood table to his right, then fumbled in the leather pocket behind the driver's seat and pulled out a round mirror. "You want more booger sugar?"

"You don't have to ask me twice." Though I was sufficiently buzzed, it was my credo never to turn down free drugs.

Doug poured a mound of coke onto the mirror and used a credit card to cut six large rails. He quickly snorted two before pausing and pointing up at the television screen. "Look. The kid's got his dick in the peephole, and he thinks those hot young things are gonna suck it. But they got the hell out of there." He was snorting and chuckling, which made it difficult to comprehend what he was saying. "It's only Balbricker in the shower now. He has no idea. Ha ha. I love this part. Look, she's got his dick in her hand and she's not letting go." Doug laughed so hard that I thought he was going to drop the mirror. I lunged forward to catch it, but he recovered his grip at the last second. "God, I love that scene. So fucking funny," he said, still chuckling. He snorted one more line before passing the mirror to me. I snorted the three remaining lines and realized that if I did any more of his blow, I was probably going to have a heart attack.

We drove for about twenty minutes before the van came to a stop and the nurse turned around in the driver's seat and said, "We're here. Are you ready to go in?"

Doug looked at him and replied curtly, "I was born ready. Now open the door, you pillow-biter." The nurse shook his head, exited the car, and walked around the vehicle to open the sliding door. He lowered Doug out of the van, and I hopped out shortly behind him. I couldn't exactly pinpoint the neighborhood we were in, but it looked like the west-side avenues off of Geary Street. We stood before a nondescript, grey travertine tile-covered storefront underneath a massive yellow plastic marquee that read, "Paradise Club. Oriental Massage. Private Bath." A neon sign that flashed the word "OPEN" hung alongside a thick grey metal door with a sliding peephole. It all made sense now. Paradise Club wasn't a dance club. It was an Asian massage parlor. I should have known that he'd take me to a "rub and tug." Doug maneuvered his wheelchair towards me and slapped my ass. "This is where the fun begins. Come on," he shouted as he rode towards the foreboding grey metal door.

"Doug, I totally appreciate this, but I'm good. It's getting late and I gotta work tomorrow." Though I had never been to a massage parlor before, I wasn't interested in visiting one that night, especially accompanied by Doug the Retard.

"What do you mean? You're not fucking going home. This is where the fun begins. What? Are you scared? Do you want to wait in the car with the homo? Maybe you two can give each other reach-arounds." Doug's nurse rolled his eyes and returned to the van.

"I guess I can go." This reminded me of high school. Here I was being peer pressured by a middle-aged man in a wheelchair. I almost expected him to make chicken-clucking noises. Reluctantly, I followed Doug to the entrance. He pressed the doorbell, and several seconds later the peephole door slid open and two eyes peered out.

"Hello, may I help you?" asked a voice with a thick Asian accent.

"Open the fucking door. We want a massage," Doug answered.

"Okay. Hold on." The peephole slid shut, a deadbolt was unlocked, and the grey door swung open to reveal a paunchy, balding Korean man in a dark blue suit standing in the doorway.

"Hello, Mr. Doug. Very good to see you again," he said, bowing slightly.

"Well, hello there, Wang." The man stepped aside and allowed us to enter a small room lit by harsh florescent lights hanging overhead. I immediately noticed five young Korean girls—who couldn't have been older than sixteen—wearing pink lingerie and sitting on metal folding chairs against a faux wood-paneled wall on the right. They were silently staring at a dance program on a small television in the corner of the room. To our left was a massive aquarium containing a variety of colorful fish, and oddly enough on top of the tank was a boombox playing the Madonna song "Like a Prayer." An older Korean woman wearing a rose gown stood behind a glass counter in the back of the room next to a younger Korean man in a dark suit who was furiously typing away into his cellphone. The woman whispered something in the young man's ear and he instantly shoved his phone into his jacket pocket. She gingerly stepped around the counter and greeted Doug with a small bow.

"Hello, Douglas. As always, it's a pleasure to see you again," the woman said demurely and with barely a trace of an accent.

"Hello, Sang-mi. You look exquisite. Who do you have for me today?"

Sang-mi gestured to her left to the five young diminutive girls staring at the tiny television. She screamed something at them in Korean, and the girls at once directed their attention towards us. "Mr. Doug, I have only the most beautiful girls for you today. Who do you fancy?"

Doug looked the girls over for a minute or two before returning his attention to Sang-mi."Is Joy here?" he asked, almost pleadingly.

"I'm very sorry, but Joy is no longer with us. We have many other beautiful girls here to please you."

Doug seemed perturbed. "I don't give a fuck. I'll take those two," he said, pointing dismissively at the two youngest-appearing girls of the five.

"Excellent choice, Mr. Doug. You will not be disappointed." Sang-mi walked over to the two girls he had selected and whispered something in Korean to them. Both girls immediately stood up, and Sang-mi adjusted the straps of their lingerie so that they hung perfectly off their tiny shoulders. With her hands on the small of their backs, she gently guided the girls towards Doug. Again she said something in Korean to them, and they both greeted Doug with a small bow.

I was still standing in the doorway trying to comprehend the weirdness of the situation. Doug shifted his wheelchair into reverse and circled around so he was facing me. "Which slope are you taking?"

"Excuse me?"

"I said which slope are you taking?"

"Uh, okay. You're talking about the girls. I'll take that one, I guess," I said, pointing to the girl nearest me. The young girl obediently stood up from her metal chair and walked toward me.

Doug laughed. "Good choice. She looks like a virgin. Go easy on her, buddy." He lifted his hand up in the air to give me a high five, but I pretended not to notice and walked towards the girl I had selected. Doug grabbed the hands of the two young girls he had picked and with a broad smile said, "Come ladies, let's have some fun." I watched him ride past the glass counter and through a plastic rainbow-beaded curtain in the back of the room. Sang-mi followed behind him, leaving me alone in the room standing awkwardly next to the teenage girl, the young man in the dark suit, and Wang, the older Korean man, who was now leaning on the glass counter smoking a cigarette.

Wang looked at me and smiled. "What are you waiting for, Doug's friend? You take the girl to a room."

"Uh, okay. Can I choose any available room, or do you have a particular room for me?" I had no idea how this operation was supposed to work.

Wang laughed and said something in Korean to the younger guy in the dark suit. Now both men were laughing. After a few seconds, Wang looked at me again and said, "Doug's friend, you take the second room on the right, okay?" He shifted his attention towards the young girl I had picked and barked something at her in Korean. She yelled in Korean back at him, and he slapped her hard across the face. The girl burst into tears.

I was shocked. "Whoa, man. Take it easy."

Wang pointed his index finger at me menacingly for a few seconds before slowly moving his finger towards the crying girl. Out of the corner of my eye, I saw the younger man in the dark suit move a few steps closer to us. Wang barked another command in Korean, and the crying girl stood up obediently, walked over to me, and grabbed my hand. Wang looked back at me and said, "Doug's friend, you go have fun now, okay?"

The young girl, still crying somewhat, pulled me towards the beaded curtain. I followed her down a hallway lit only with red Christmas lights to the second door on the right. She opened the door and motioned for me to enter. The room was barely larger than a walk-in closet and contained only an old massage table with gaping holes in the red vinyl covering and a small stereo sitting on top of a metal folding chair. The girl had stopped crying and sullenly handed me a towel that was lying on top of the massage table. She dutifully walked over to the stereo and pressed the play button. The Lionel Richie song "Ballerina Girl" began to play softly, which only served to make this exceedingly unerotic situation that much more unerotic. I strongly considered handing the girl fifty dollars and leaving, but I was worried that the old Korean man might do something horrible to her.

"Hi, my name's Dave," I said, trying my best not to sound nervous. She looked at me blankly. I tried again. "My name's Dave," I said, pointing at my chest. "What's your name?"

The girl smiled politely and moved towards me. She began unbuttoning the top buttons of my shirt. I gently pushed her back and held her by her shoulders and said once again, "My name's Dave. What's your name?" She obviously did not speak English. The girl stepped back and pulled the straps of her lingerie over her shoulders and let the entire garment fall to the floor, leaving her standing there completely nude. Though she was incredibly attractive, I felt unnerved being aroused by a girl who had to have been several years short of the legal age in this country. And she had one of the largest bushes I had ever seen. For some reason, I was surprised that Korean girls were so hairy down there. The naked girl again approached me and started unbuttoning my shirt. I stepped back with my hand outstretched, motioning to her that I could remove my clothes myself, and she stood there motionless, watching me disrobe. I wrapped the towel around my waist and carefully placed my pile of clothes next to the stereo. She pointed to the table, and as I lay across it on my stomach, I struggled to dismiss the thought of how many men that day had ejaculated on that same table. She straddled my ass and kneaded my back with her tiny but powerful fingers. It felt amazing, and I closed my eyes and for the first time that day began to feel somewhat relaxed when suddenly I heard a man shouting in one of the other rooms.

133

It sounded a lot like Doug's voice but it was hard to tell. I arched my back up, but the girl pushed me down, shaking her head from side to side. The shouting soon subsided, and she continued to massage my back for the next ten minutes before sliding off of me and urging me to flip over. I complied and rolled over onto my back, noticing that the Lionel Richie song "Say You, Say Me" was now playing. The girl massaged my thighs and slowly moved her hands upwards toward the towel. Without warning, she reached under the towel and firmly gripped my tumescent penis. Not anticipating this sudden grope, I sat up and held the towel firmly over my crotch.

"Whoa, what are you doing? Don't do that." The girl just stood there looking at me confused. "No, I don't want you to do that," I repeated, waving my finger at her admonishingly. She smiled and tried to grab the towel. I gripped her shoulder with my right hand and gently pushed her away. "No, that's not cool. Just a massage. That's it." She giggled and reached for the towel again.

"Tug tug," she said, still giggling.

"No. No tug tug. Just massage." She wasn't listening and instead snatched the corner of the towel and gave it a hard pull. I pulled back with enough force that it wrenched free from her grip. I slipped off the table, still holding the towel over my crotch, and repeated myself using a more authoritative tone, "No, I don't want a tug tug."

"Yes, tug tug," she said, now laughing.

"No," I shouted the word like I would to a puppy that just shit on the living room carpet. "No tug tugs." She ran around the massage table and tried to grab the towel. I pushed her hand away and ran backwards to the other side of the table. She chased after me, laughing hysterically, while trying to snatch the towel from my hands. "Stop. You need to stop this right now," I shouted, running away from her. We circled the table two times before I stepped to the right corner of the room and used the chair with the stereo on it as a bulwark. The naked girl stood facing me with the chair standing between us. She made swift reaches around the chair, trying to grab the towel, the whole time yelling, "tug tug" and laughing. We probably would have continued this perverted cat-and-mouse game for some time had the door to the room not swung open to reveal Mr. Wang standing there with blood pouring out of his nose. His face was flushed and it was obvious that he was really pissed off. Loud and furious shouts emanated from one of the other rooms down the red hallway.

"You get Mr. Doug and get the fuck out of here. Now!" Wang screeched, spittle forming in the corners of his mouth. He delivered a salvo of what I thought were obscenities at me, but I couldn't really tell because he was speaking in Korean, and then he slapped the young girl so hard that she fell backwards and knocked over the massage table. Wang rushed towards her as if he was about to give her a hard kick, but I stepped in front of him, still holding the towel over my crotch.

"Yo, chill. Calm down, dude. I'll get Doug. We'll get out of here. Just calm down and let me put my fucking pants on."

"You get the fuck out of here. Now!" he yelled, sharply emphasizing "now." Then he turned towards the sobbing girl and viciously berated her in Korean.

Without bothering to put on my underwear, I hastily shoved my right leg into my trousers and almost fell over. I had to use the chair for balance before trying the other leg. The whole time Wang eyed me distrustfully, not bothering to wipe the blood streaming from his nose. The front of his white shirt was covered in dark red splotches. "Hey, Mr.

Wang. I don't really know Doug, and whatever he did does not involve me. Okay?" I had no idea the severity of Doug's infraction, and I was trying to vindicate myself as best I could.

Wang dismissed my caveat and glared at me before shouting again in broken English, "You take Mr. Doug and get the fuck out of here!"

"Okay, that's cool. We're outta here." I put my hands in the air in a defensive pose, trying to show him that I meant no harm as I bent down and grabbed my shirt off the floor. I threw it on without fastening the buttons and quickly slipped on my shoes. Wang was still screaming at the crying girl, but as soon as he noticed that I was dressed, he grabbed my arm, pulled me out of the room, and led me down the hallway towards an open door at the end. The shouting was much louder in the hallway, and I could hear a woman screaming and Doug cursing at her. When we got to the doorway, Wang shoved me inside.

"You get Mr. Doug and get the fuck out!"

"Okay. okay, we're go…" The words froze in my mouth as I gazed upon the chaotic scene playing out before me. One of the Korean masseuses was lying in a heap on the floor, crying hysterically, her face and hands covered in blood; the other girl was straddling Doug's wheelchair, clawing at him like a wild animal, screeching in Korean; and the younger Korean man in the dark suit had Doug in a headlock and was trying to pull him and his wheelchair towards the doorway. Doug was yelling, "Get off me, you gook bitch," and holding on for dear life to the leg of the massage table. Even though there was a naked girl on top of him, I could see that he was also naked and that there was some type of plastic pump device between his legs. Wang shoved me out of his way and began pummeling Doug's face while cursing at him in Korean. Oddly, what I recall most about the situation was the Styx song "Lady" playing on the portable stereo that lay overturned on the ground. The song seemed like the perfect soundtrack at the time. I stood there in shock for what seemed like ten minutes but was probably less than ten seconds. With most violent situations, time ceases to be linear and all events seem to occur in chorus. I stood in the doorway, paralyzed, surveying the bedlam happening in slow motion before me, struggling to determine my role in resolving it when the adrenalin coursing through my body triggered its natural fight-or-flight response. Instinctively, I turned around and fled from the room. I bolted full speed down the hallway lit with the red Christmas lights and through the plastic rainbow-beaded curtain and out the grey metal door without once looking back. I didn't even check to see if I was being followed. At that point, I just wanted to get the fuck out of there.

The cool night air barely soothed my trembling body, and I took several deep breaths before walking briskly up the street away from Paradise Club. When I had felt that I had reached a safe distance, I looked over my shoulder to see if I was being followed. Even though no one was chasing after me, I was still scared shitless and walked as fast as I could without appearing conspicuous. After about two blocks, I stopped and lit a cigarette and noticed Doug's Mercedes parked across the street. I crossed the street and knocked on the tinted driver's window. Nothing happened. I knocked again, this time a bit harder, and the window rolled down about halfway. The nurse who resembled John Waters sat in the driver's seat holding his cellphone listlessly in his right hand. He was visibly annoyed at having his conversation interrupted.

"What?"

"Umm. You might want to go in there and fetch Doug. Something serious is going down. I don't know what he did, but they're not very happy with him."

"Fuck him," he replied, and rolled up the tinted black window.

I stood there staring at the closed window for a few seconds before backing away from the van and heading up the street. I didn't have the faintest clue where I was, but I wasn't all that concerned. San Francisco isn't a very large city and sooner or later I was bound to find a cab somewhere. But I did make one resolution that evening: the next time I encounter a disabled man lying on a bathroom floor, I'm leaving him there.

The Birthday Boy

I sincerely enjoyed emceeing the birthday and bachelor parties at all the strip clubs that I have worked at because these are prime occasions for mockery. Not only is the DJ encouraged to embarrass the bachelor boy, it's practically required by his peers and the club's management. It's the only instance on the job where the DJ is expected to be a complete and utter bastard. I must admit that it was a lot of fun. There was nothing off limits, and I had absolutely no misgivings about personally insulting the bachelor boy. The procedure at most clubs was essentially the same for bachelor parties and birthday parties. At the Doll House and most other strip clubs, bachelor parties were a free service provided by the club as long as the bachelor or birthday boy showed proof of his age or his upcoming marriage. Typically, a member of the bachelor party would come to the DJ booth and ask me about how the bachelor parties worked at the club. I persuaded him to purchase one for the bachelor even though I knew full well that the party was offered as a courtesy. But by the time most bachelor parties arrived at a strip club, they were so intoxicated, and eager to humiliate the bachelor, that they would pay me whatever I asked, which was usually around $200. I didn't have qualms about lying to customers because they were usually too drunk to realize it, and if I didn't do it, another employee would have taken their money. Regardless, I made sure that they purchased the bachelor boy a memorable experience. I'd wait for an appropriate time to announce the bachelor's name and put him onstage with his back against the pole surrounded by ten to fifteen dancers. The dancers then took his shirt off and used his belt to bind his hands together behind the pole. With Motley Crue's "Girls, Girls, Girls" blaring from the speakers and his friends jeering at him, the strippers formed a single-file line and each one of them had a chance to straddle the inebriated bachelor and shove their tits in his face. Some of the more sadistic dancers climbed to the top of the pole and slid down hard onto the poor guy's lap and bounced up and down a few times. Others bent the guy over, grabbed a hold of his underwear, and pulled until it tore, giving him the most painful wedgie he had ever experienced. All this was done for the delight of his companions. Amidst all the sadism, I delivered the standard cheesedick DJ bachelor party lines:

"Hey, ladies, did you know that the bachelor boy is twenty-seven years old and still a virgin? So let's pop that cherry tonight."

"Hey, (name of bachelor). Do you remember your first blowjob? Yeah. Well, how did you get the taste out of your mouth?"

"His last two wives divorced him because they couldn't find his dick. It's a good thing his fiancé is blind, he can just use his finger."

A DJ can also get a positive reaction from the crowd by mocking his fiancé's weight, peg leg, facial hair, penis, and so on. There's a plethora of good material available. It all hinges on the delivery. Frequently, the best man would provide me with a list of embarrassing personal details and inside jokes. That facilitated matters, because now all I had to do was simply read the comments, embellish them a bit, and they were guaranteed to make the crowd roar with laughter. Once each girl had her chance to punish the bachelor boy, we untied him and asked the crowd to give him a round of applause for being a good sport. At some clubs, I'd cajole the bachelor to do a little dance for the girls onstage to some ridiculous song like "YMCA" or "I'm Too Sexy." This was a surefire crowd-pleaser, and I could usually encourage the intoxicated bachelor to do a pole trick for the audience. At the very end, one of the managers would give him a T-shirt, porn, or a shot glass as a souvenir. It was the least we could do after that embarrassing spectacle.

I did one birthday at the Doll House that still vexes me to this day. I'll never forget the poor eighteen-year-old kid whose older brother forced him to go onstage and celebrate, as he so aptly put it, "entering into manhood." It was a Friday night, and there were about twenty-two girls on the rotation and a roomful of miserly perverts not purchasing dances and hardly tipping. In other words, it was a typical evening. The girls were annoyed because they were getting naked for free, and I was forced to put them onstage for a pointless Red Light Special every twenty minutes in a feeble attempt to raise the sagging dance count. During one of these futile specials, a large, bespectacled man with a freshly buzzed haircut and a seriously pockmarked face approached the DJ booth. He told me that his younger brother was going to turn eighteen at midnight and wanted to know if we did anything special for birthdays. His haircut and harsh, unyielding tone clued me in that I was dealing with a military man.

"Sir, are you a member of the Armed Forces?" I inquired.

"I'm a US Marine currently on leave."

"Your haircut gave it away. Since you're a Marine, I'm going to hook you up with a great show for your little bro over there. We support the troops here at the Doll House. For you, it'll only be $100."

The Marine was quite grateful and eagerly handed me a crisp $100 bill. Military men make easy marks, and most tend to spend a great deal of money at strip clubs. Either they are too hard up to realize they are being hustled or too drunk to care. He waited by the booth till I announced the next girl, shook my hand firmly, and said, "My brother is an eighteen-year-old virgin, and it's about damn time he became a man."

I laughed out loud when he said this and reassured him, "Don't worry, soldier, it will be my mission to make sure the girls pop his cherry tonight." I continued chuckling but stopped abruptly when I realized that the Marine wasn't laughing.

He grimaced and spoke in a solemn tone. "While I see the humor, this is no laughing matter. My brother's virginity is of deep concern to my family. We think he may be a homosexual."

This almost caused me to begin laughing again, but I could tell that the Marine was deadly serious. I was at a loss. Really, I didn't know what to tell him. Not to mention, I was trying with all my might to suppress an outburst of laughter. He stood there—arms akimbo—staring at me like a terrorist at a military tribunal.

"You know, it's not uncommon for some guys to lose their virginity in their twenties, and for all you know, he might be saving it for marriage."

The Marine frowned deeply and replied, "Bullshit. My brother's a faggot, and you know it."

"Hey, I'm just a strip club DJ, not a psychologist. But don't worry, I'll make sure the ladies take care of your brother."

He nodded, slapped my shoulder, and walked away from the booth. Unable to suppress it any longer, I crouched down and burst into a fit of laughter. I seriously hoped his brother was gay because then he probably wouldn't be forced to join the military like the rest of the male members of his family. But honestly, I couldn't care less. Midnight was about a half hour away, and I continued running the show while scanning the audience members for the Marine and his alleged homosexual sibling. The pair sat stone-faced in the back corner of the room, not even attempting conversation. It was more than obvious that this visit to the strip club was not the gay brother's idea. The kid had a youthful, feminine appearance. He was extremely thin, and his freshly shaved scalp made him look a bit like a young Sinéad O'Connor. In hindsight, I never asked the Marine for an ID, so as far as I knew the kid could have been fifteen. But it was obvious by his facial expression and nervous fidgeting that the kid was scared shitless. This excursion to the nudie bar was going to be a traumatic experience for him, one he'll no doubt share with his therapist years later. He paid no attention to the writhing naked bodies onstage. Instead, his eyes darted nervously around the room, and his hand trembled like a Parkinson's patient as he gingerly lifted his soda glass to his lips. The kid was so agitated that he dropped his glass on the floor twice while trying to rest it on the oblong side table. The callous Marine was either oblivious to his brother's distress or trained to ignore it, and he focused his complete attention on the girl on the main stage. He analyzed her every move with military precision as if he was waiting for her to pull out a revolver and endanger his life or the lives of his comrades. That poor kid. I could tell by looking at him that he would have rather masturbated with a handful of thumbtacks than be put on a stage with these ladies. The kid sat there nervously playing with a coin,

143

counting the seconds to his impending doom, much like a condemned murderer with a rosary clutched within his sweaty palms awaiting his inevitable date with the mercy seat. The Marine was firm in his conviction that this was the only way to cure his brother of his homosexuality, and he forced his brother to sit in the strip club like a normal, heterosexual male and enjoy the sight of naked females whether he liked it or not. Finally, the clock struck midnight and it was time for his brother to enter into manhood. I announced for all the girls to stand by the main stage and then excitedly called out the name of the Birthday Boy.

"Well, guess what, ladies and gents? We have a Birthday Boy in the house! Billy Clemens. I need you on the main stage."

I pressed the play button, and 50 Cent's "In Da Club" blared from the speakers. One of the bouncers hoisted a chair onto the stage, and another escorted the hapless wretch to his inevitable fate. The kid walked slowly and carefully as if his hands and legs were manacled.

"Ladies and gents, let's make a little noise out there for Billy. It's his birthday, for fuck's sake."

The audience erupted into a loud round of applause and cheers. I don't quite know the reason I made the next comment. It might have been to rouse the crowd or to incite the strippers, but for some nefarious reason, I gleefully announced:

"Hey, ladies, you might want to give him the special treatment. His brother told me he's a virgin and that we have to pop his cherry tonight."

This made the crowd roar with laughter, which soon devolved into catcalls and whistles when the dancers walked onto the stage.

"Eighteen years old and still a virgin. Well, that's gonna change tonight," I said, my voice booming over the microphone.

The dancers ripped the kid's shirt off, exposing his hairless, bony chest. They unlatched his belt, released it from the loops, and used it to bind his shaking hands behind his back. I scanned the wildly cheering audience for the Marine whom I expected to see in a front-row seat participating in the festivities. Since he had forced his brother to endure this torture, the least he could do was provide some moral support. I found him sitting in the same seat in the back corner with the same stone-faced countenance that he had had before. Oddly, the Marine didn't seem to be enjoying this experience any more than his brother. About midway through the song, I noticed that the boy's complexion had blanched into a pale, ghostly white. The girls filed into a single line, and each one of them bounced on his lap in turn. Perhaps they were feeling a bit more sadistic or hateful because the customers were spending so little money on them, but regardless of the reason, they were merciless on that particular night. They took their full collective wrath out on that kid. I felt deep pangs of sympathy for the kid. Some of the girls climbed to the top of the pole and mercilessly slid down on his small knees with such force that it made the chair bounce on the stage. Others climbed onto his lap and smashed his face into their ample, oily bosoms. It appeared as if they were beating the boy with their breasts. A right. Then a left. And then another right-left combination. And then, bam. Knockout. The kid's head smashed against the brass pole behind him so hard that you could hear it over the music. The crowd loved it. They were cheering, clapping, and tossing crumpled dollar bills at the girls and their whipping boy. Amid the thrashing, I threw in an occasional "That had to hurt" or "Damn, I'm glad it's not my Birthday," but I was losing my enthusiasm. The kid's body seemed to quiver within its restraints, and I could see tears streaming from his eyes. The boy was so scared that he was actually sobbing. I had never emceed a birthday show like this. I wanted to put a stop to the thrashing, but the harpies weren't quite satiated yet. One of them bent the kid over and held his shoulders down while another grasped the elastic of his tightie-whities. She yanked so hard that it tore the elastic clean off his underwear and the boy let out a lingering wail. At this, the girls started laughing and smacking his ass even harder than normal. The kid was hunched over, bawling, and his whole body seemed to tremble with each slap. I cut the song short because it was time for this kid's humiliation to end.

"Ladies and gents, how 'bout a big round of applause for the Birthday Boy! Happy Birthday, Billy! Thanks for coming to the Doll House tonight."

The crowd clapped and cheered while the dancers loosened the belt straps around the kid's hands and helped him to his feet. Then I heard a high-pitched female voice shriek:

"Oh my god. He peed his pants."

146

This caused all the strippers to turn around, look at the kid, and break out into shrill fits of laughter. The entire room seemed to point their index fingers accusingly towards the stage as the audience convulsed into a tsunami of laughter. The sniveling boy stood there mortified under the flashing white, red, and blue lights, staring down at the darkening stain on the crotch of his light blue jeans. Everyone in the room, with the exception of the Marine and myself, hissed and jeered. I hastily flipped on the next song, turned up the volume to drown out the jeers, and ran a 2-for-1 dance special. The laughter soon eroded into a chuckle, and the girls started making their way around the room in a vain attempt to find someone to buy a lap dance. Meanwhile, the Marine took this opportunity to snatch his brother by the arm and forcefully haul his quivering frame off the stage and out of the club. I half expected him to demand his money back, and I was more than willing to return it. I felt horrible. This kid's first sexual experience with women involved a savage beating and public humiliation. If he wasn't gay before, he was definitely gay now. Or more likely, he'd become a twisted serial killer. As the Marine walked by the booth dragging his sobbing gay brother, I mustered an apologetic expression on my face and reached into my pocket to retrieve his money. With his brother's elbow in his death grip, he glanced over at me, muttered a terse "Thank you," and quickly exited the club. I shoved the bill back in my pocket and was overwrought by these unsettling feelings of remorse and bewilderment. At the end of the night, I used that crisp $100 bill to purchase drugs. I had to get rid of it.

Fiona

I loathed emceeing the girl-on-girl shows and would've gladly given up a weekend shift to avoid them. These shows occurred at Foxys once or twice a night on Friday and Saturday night shifts, and only certain managers would force us to do them. And by certain managers, I mean Pepper. Pepper fervently enjoyed the girl-on-girl shows. If he had enough volunteers, he'd have happily ran five shows a night. Luckily, he rarely had volunteers. The truth was that the dancers either despised doing the shows or were absolutely terrified of them. Pepper, however, was cunning and persuasive and always seemed to be able to extort or bribe the girls into participating. He might not have had much of a formal education, but he was definitely streetwise. Shedding his abrasive demeanor, he'd approach a dancer with a sensitive, almost paternal mien. He smiled widely, massaged her shoulders, and whispered softly:

"Damn, baby. You lookin' good tonight. Ummm. Ummm. For real tho. You lookin' damn good. And you smell like a bouquet of the finest red roses. Girl, I need you to do Pepper a little favor. You want to be in that girl-on-girl show tonight? That's cool if you don't. It's just that I finna make sure you'll make bank, baby. You know you owe me one."

After he delivered his opening lines, most dancers, especially the seasoned ones, would look at him with an expression of disbelief and respond with a curt, "Hell no! Nigga, I don't owe you shit."

But Pepper anticpated this response, and once his initial anger had subsided, he looked the girl over once or twice, smacked his lips together, and calmly replied, "Damn, girl. You don't need to be like that. Pepper's jus' tryin' to help you make some money. Now I know you showed up twenty minutes late tonight. Technically, I'm supposed to charge you a late fee, but we don't have to go there if you help a nigga out."

This ploy worked like a charm on the less experienced dancers, and they'd accept his offer to avoid eighty dollars in late fees. Whereas the seasoned dancers would still reject the offer because they'd done these shows before and had concluded that the compensation was not worth the effort and humiliation. To persuade them, Pepper had to resort to harsher tactics. He shifted into "angry pimp" mode and looked them directly in the eye when he spoke.

"Damn, girl, why you disrespectin' me like that? You know I'm here to make you money. Listen. If you don't do the show tonight, I might have to fire you for smoking herb in the dressin' room. I don't want to do that, but you ain't givin' Pepper much of a choice."

The accused dancer immediately denied his accusation. "Pepper, I wasn't smoking herb. Who told you that? These bitches lyin'. For real. I ain't never smoked herb in the dressin' room."

"Girl, I had three ladies come up to me and tell me this, and you know we have a camera back there. Videotape don't lie. You want to take a walk upstairs and see fo' yo'self? Listen, girl, we don't have to go there. I don't want to fire you. You make me too much money. I'd be hurtin' myself by doin' that."

Most of the girls, including the veterans, were too dense to realize that it was illegal for management to install video cameras in the girl's dressing room. At this point, Pepper had them, and when they cried and confessed, he embraced them and ran his fingers through their hair and said soothingly, "Damn, baby. You don't need to cry. But you do look fine when you cryin' tho. We can forget about all of this if you do me one small favor tonight. Fo' real. I'll make this go away."

It amused me that strippers, who are hustlers by their nature, would fold so easily to such an unfounded allegation. Regardless, this tactic almost always proved to be successful for him. He now had his performers for the girl-on-girl show. I don't think Pepper truly believed that these shows were successful promotions as much as he derived some type of misogynistic pleasure from watching two desperate women shove dildos up each other's openings. In short, that was what the girl-on-girl show consisted of: two forlorn strippers on a stage surrounded by screaming men chucking crumpled dollar bills at them while they dispassionately shoved dildos up each other's vaginas and assholes. It was a deplorable scene that appealed to the lowest common denominator of male sexuality. I found nothing erotic about these performances. At least one of the participants was either frozen in fear or so high on heroin or GHB that she just lay there while her partner sodomized her with a lubed dildo, and a crowd of whooping eighteen-year-old males pelted them with dollar bills. I found the whole scene revolting, and as much as I would try to sound enthusiastic as the emcee, I just couldn't bring myself to do it. I didn't have an issue feigning enthusiasm during the Red Light Specials, but the girl-on-girl shows bothered me. Pepper was well aware of my lack of gusto, and once the show started, he'd walk over to the DJ booth and call me "faggot" or a "pussy," grab the portable microphone, and take over the announcer responsibility. I was more than willing to relinquish the job to him regardless of whether he thought I was less of a man. In reality, I really didn't give a shit what Pepper thought of me. I gladly handed over the mic and stepped outside for a cigarette break for the four songs that comprised the show. Occasionally, I wasn't given a choice and had to emcee the whole show, but usually Pepper preferred to be the emcee and relegate me to a supporting role. It was eerie to observe Pepper shed his false paternal, benevolent persona and transform into the shameless deviant that was his true character. His eyes lit up with sadistic excitation, and his tone was forceful and commanding. He genuinely enjoyed being the ringmaster of this debauched spectacle and directing the girls to debase themselves in front of a crowd of drunk, salivating meatheads. Pepper definitely was skilled at inciting a crowd, I'll give him that. He literally stoked them into a feeding frenzy, each one fighting for a position at the main stage to whip crumpled dollar bills at the miserable perfomers. With 2 Live Crew's "Me So Horny" blaring through the club's speakers, Pepper bellowed:

"Damn. Two bitches on the main stage ready to get nasty wit' ya. Let's go, fellas. Come on. I said let's go. Get on up to the front row for one hell of a show. The bigger the bills, the harder the thrills. Use those dollars to make them holler. I want to hear these bitches scream. Yeah, baby. You like it like that. They getting down and dirty up there. You nasty girl. Damn. Slap that ass. That's what I'm talkin' about. You can do it, put yo ass into it. Ummm. Lemme hear you make some fuckin' noise out there. Come on now. You heard about the 69. How 'bout the 88? That's when you put four fingers in the pussy and four fingers in the asshole. Double fistin' that shit. Now that's what I came here for. Damn."

I would occasionally chime in with a "damn" or "goddamn" or "we love it when she does that," but for the most part, I let Pepper emcee the show on his own. These shows bothered me, and I breathed a heavy sigh of relief when Pepper was thwarted and couldn't find any willing participants. Though he'd attempt to cajole every dancer who showed up that night, sometimes he had no choice but to cancel the show.

The only dancer I ever worked with who managed to foil Pepper was a diminutive woman named Fiona. She was a genuinely evil person who cared little for the well-being of others, including her own offspring. Rumor had it that at the age of twenty-six, she had been married twice and given birth to three children who she had not seen in over six years. Fiona was a natural hustler. The hustle was a component of her genetic makeup; it flowed through her veins. She followed a matrilineal line of sex workers: her grandmother was a prostitute, her mother was a prostitute, and she had become a prostitute at the age of thirteen when she ran away from home. Originally from Panama, she had moved to the States when she was seventeen and had worked as a prostitute and a stripper in clubs across the country. I wouldn't describe her as attractive. I thought she bore a striking resemblance to Sylvester Stallone if he was a 4'10" brunette with massive, surgically-enhanced 36-DD breasts. Yet, she did very well at Foxys, so I assume there exist some men who find this type of woman appealing. Either that, or she charged less than the other girls for blowjobs.

Fiona detested the stage and usually tried to bribe me to remove her name from the dancer rotation. She experienced severe birthing complications with two of her children that resulted in massive scarring across her lower abdomen. Though she expertly concealed her blemishes with exotic scarves wrapped tightly around her waist, one could see that she was deeply self-conscious of her body. Bribery of the DJ is a frequent occurrence at all strip clubs. It's a huge risk because if he gets caught, he will be severely reprimanded by management or possibly terminated. Depending on the amount of the bribe, my relationship with the dancer, and the manager on duty, I usually took the risk. I didn't like Fiona much at all and she was well aware of this. She was also aware that management paid little attention to the stage rotation, and it was completely up to the DJ who danced that night. Therefore, our relationship was solely opportunistic. If she gave me $50 at the beginning of her shift and another $50 at the end, I would remove her name from the list and she'd avoid the stage completely. Fiona also had a notorious meth habit and was repeatedly tardy for her shifts, which gave Pepper an advantage when negotiating her participation in the girl-on-girl shows. She was typically forty-five minutes late for every shift and had to pay the regular stage fee of $50 and an additional fine of $80 for being late. And not to mention the $50 that she gave to me to take her name off the stage rotation. That's a lot of money for a meth-addicted stripper to come up with at the beginning of her shift. As soon as she crept into the club, Pepper swooped on her, flashed his gold-toothed smile, wrapped his arms tight around her tiny shoulders, and smugly said:

"Damn, girl. You didn't think you could sneak past Pepper? Come on now. You know me better than that. If you want to work tonight, you owe me $130."

Fiona squirmed out of his grip, sneered, and continued walking towards the dressing room completely ignoring him. This enraged Pepper, and he yelled, "Damn, bitch! Don't you ever turn your back on me when I'm talking to you. Now get yo ass over here. Listen. You're late. Now I can make you pay $130 to work tonight, or I can make you pay nuthin'. Whatcha want: $130 or nuthin'? That's right. You want to pay nuthin'. I want you to be in that girl-on-girl show tonight and I'll forget about yo late fee and I'll even forget about yo stage fee. Know what I'm sayin'?"

He knew that he had her. Pepper often said that "managing bitches is like playing poker. You gotta know when you have the upper hand, and you betta lay down that shit, nigga. Damn." He could tell he had the upper hand by the fury burning in her eyes. "A bitch's eyes never lie, and if they do, you want to leave that bitch alone. She'll cut yo dick off. I ain't lyin' about that. Damn." Fiona had no other choice but to pay her fees to the house—which I highly doubt she had—or do the girl-on-girl show and pay nothing. She reluctantly opted for the latter.

"Okay, Pepper. I'll do the show tonight," she relented with a sinister smile.

Fiona was a born hustler and devised her own method of excluding herself from all future girl-on-girl shows. Her partner that night was a young Hawaiian girl named Kiana who had been stripping at Foxys for less than a month. She had also arrived late for her shift that night, and Pepper had easily manipulated her into doing the show to avoid the late fee. She had absolutely no idea what lay in store for her. It was difficult to watch. With her mouth twisted into a devious smile throughout the two-song ordeal, Fiona brutally sodomized Kiana with a large dildo, spat in her face, pulled out some of her hair, and smacked her ass with such force that the pitiful girl was left with a red handprint for the next three days. Kiana fled the stage in tears while the crowd roared with hoots, laughter, and applause. After this heartless display of aggression, there was not a single dancer in the club who would dare go onstage with Fiona. Even the new hires had heard rumors of Fiona's cruelty and refused to be in a show with her. To Pepper's dismay, she had disqualified herself for lack of a willing partner. And knowing that the girls feared her, she would constantly taunt Pepper by volunteering to be in a show or innocently inquiring whether there was one scheduled for that night. He ignored her jibes and pretended that he was working on some pressing business matter all the while muttering hateful, misogynistic comments under his breath.

Play Something Dancy

In my professional opinion, I would have to say that the music is the most crucial element of the show. Well, that is, aside from the tits. The music is not only used to manipulate crowd reaction, it sets the overall ambiance of the club, and that's the reason the DJs are required to spin songs that are up-tempo, energetic, and, most importantly, recognizable to the audience.

The DJ must maintain a festive, party atmosphere throughout the night as to ensure that all patrons have a positive experience and return to the club in the future.

I had a manager who made all of the DJs repeat this mantra three times every night shift to make sure we understood how to run the show. It's news to me that shelling out nine dollars for a domestic beer and paying a stripper exorbitant amounts of money only to be left sexually frustrated could be considered a positive experience. Perhaps a positive experience is subjective. Most upscale clubs strictly regulate the style and tempo of the music to manipulate the mood of the crowd. The management requires the DJ to play house or trance music that's at least 120 beats per minute, classic rock, current Top 40 rock, and, sadly, a surplus of eighties music. These clubs target a specific demographic: Caucasian businessmen within the thirty- to fifty-year age range. A portly Causcasian man with a disposable income is a strip club owner's wet dream. These are the people who can afford to purchase VIP-Room lap dances, eagerly reach for their wallets when asked to buy a dancer a glass of Cristal, and annoyingly, love to listen to eighties music. The club's owners had done their market research or employed someone to do it for them and ordered their DJs to spin music that's enjoyed by their target audience. Conversely, at lower-tier clubs, music is not as much of an issue, and the DJ tends to have more liberty in selecting songs. At the Doll House and Foxys, we were allowed to play music ranging from Slayer to The Notorious BIG. There was much more diversity in race and age amongst the patrons, and this was the music that they listened to.

Regardless of the status of the club, all people are affected in some way by the music blasting through the club's speakers. Music is a very emotionally charged form of expression that often has a deep personal meaning or association for the listener. I've often surmised how the Déjà Vu strip clubs located across the country chose their moniker. Why the name Déjà Vu? In my mind, it's based on the sensory recollections of the customer invoked by the dancers as well as other factors, such as the background music. For example, a customer walks into a strip club, a twenty-year-old dancer sits down alongside him, and she casually initiates a conversation. While engrossed in stimulating discourse about Zodiac signs or the song she just danced to, the customer takes a deep look at her and suddenly realizes that she reminds him of his girlfriend from college or his wife when they first started dating. Déjà vu. A patron sips his overpriced domestic brew and casually observes the dancer onstage. He briefly diverts his attention from her for a moment and realizes that she is dancing to the song "Ready For Love" by the critically acclaimed arena rock outfit, Bad Company. Pausing for a brief moment of reminiscence, he recalls how he lost his virginity to that song many years ago. Déjà vu. In reality, they probably chose the name based on a recurring venereal disease that the owner caught from the dancers at one of his clubs. But it really doesn't matter how that company came up with their name. My point is that music can have a deeply emotive, nostalgic affect on the listener, and any decent DJ recognizes this fact and selects music accordingly. Music selection is essential at any club, particularly a strip club. Yet, a strip club DJ not only has to select music for the audience, but also has to select music for the dancer. And this is the most difficult part of the job. Your manager is constantly telling you to play upbeat music that is recognizable to the audience.

"Play to the money," he growls as he exhales thick plume of smoke from his Kool cigarette, his forked tongue darting in and out of his mouth.

Management's philosophy is that the music should be aimed towards the big spenders, the high rollers, and the money crowd. I must admit they had a healthy amount of reason behind their rhyme. If the high rollers are comfortable, they will spend more money. And the club's top priority is money. The problem is that most strippers couldn't care less about the livelihood of the club and want to dance to music of their preference. And nine times out of ten, their preference sucks. All strip club DJs can attest that most strippers have atrocious taste in music, but they are the ones giving us a $20 tip at the end of the night. DJs hardly receive minimum wage from the club. The majority of our income is based on the generosity of the dancers. And their tips can range anywhere from $5 to $20 to even $50 or more per dancer depending on how much they like your music selection, how much they like you personally, or what drug you've dealt to them on that particular evening.

159

And therein lies the strip club DJ conundrum: Do you play music for the crowd and your managers, or do you play music for the dancers who tip you well?

I strove to achieve a healthy balance between the two divergent forces, but this task was far from simple. While the managers are calling you on the radio, screaming about the lack of energy in the room, the stripper in the DJ booth is requesting a Portishead song because she feels tired. To the managers, a dancer's musical preference is irrelevant because a girl can get naked to any song. And I agree with this statement, to a point. The customers spend excessive amounts of money on the dancers and on drinks and food, and the DJ should placate them with the music they want to hear. However, the dancer has to disrobe in front of a throng of drooling perverts and should be allowed to feel as comfortable and as sexy as possible while she is onstage. Allow me to illustrate this conundrum with a common strip club DJ scenario:

It's Saturday night and the club is packed. In fact, there's a line outside twenty-five-deep of people waiting to get in. The stripper currently onstage is dancing to ACDC's "You Shook Me All Night Long," and the crowd is singing along, moving their heads, slapping their thighs, and covering the stage in crumpled dollar bills. They love the energy and the familiarity of the ACDC song. It's obvious that we have a rock crowd in the house tonight. The next dancer on rotation comes to the DJ booth to request a couple songs for her set. She requests R. Kelly's "Bump and Grind" because his music makes her feel sexy. If the DJ plays the R. Kelly song, he's going to decimate the energy in the room, lose the entire crowd, and consequently, invoke the wrath of his manager. On the other hand, if he doesn't play the song, then he's going to anger the dancer and forsake his tip. Keep in mind that this is only an issue if the dancer is a good tipper. In that case, I wouldn't outright refuse to play her song. Rather I would attempt to convince her to choose a more upbeat song that will please both the crowd and the managers. Like a shrewd diplomat, a seasoned strip club DJ knows how to use a combination of charisma, charm, and flattery to achieve his aims.

"Baby, 'Bump and Grind' is a great song, but if we play that right now, we're gonna kill the vibe. We got a rock crowd in here tonight. I'd recommend some Motley Crue or Guns N' Roses."

"But I don't know them."

"I know you don't. But look at the money on that stage. If you play a slow song right now, everyone's going to leave the front row and return to their tables. We'll play 'Bump and Grind' on your next set."

"You think so? Okay. I guess play whatever you want."

"Trust me. You're so sexy that you can dance to anything."

I want the dancer's tip, but I don't want to lose the crowd in order to get it. I've found that if you slant your speech in terms of finance, most dancers react favorably. Like the owners of the club, they want to make as much money as possible. She ends up dancing to a rock song, making good tips onstage, the energy in the room remains intact, and the managers are content. At the end of the night, she thanks me for helping her make money and gives me a good tip. Everyone wins. This technique worked for most cases, in particular on the novice dancers. I didn't worry about the seasoned dancers because they knew not to request slower music during peak hours, especially on weekend nights. Achieving equilibrium between the managers and the dancers with music selection is by no means a simple feat but a necessary one, if you want to keep your job and make a lot of money at the same time.

Some dancers were very particular about their music and would tell me their selection early in the night, hours before they had to go onstage. We had erasable boards in the booth, and I wrote their song selections on the board next to their name. I had to write it because I smoked far too much marijuana to remember the names of every song that a dancer requested. And heaven forfend, the DJ accidentally plays the wrong song, the dancer would feel personally violated. Their reaction was absurd and completely unwarranted. On occasion, I'd forget to write a dancer's song title down and would pick another song within her preferred genre. She'd walk onstage, hear the first few notes of the substituted song, and stare with this incredulous expression up towards the DJ booth. It was as if I had flung a ball of my own feces, like a wild primate, and hit her dead center in the chest. The unprofessional dancers would refuse to dance altogether and yell at the DJ to change the "fucking song." If this occurred, I'd completely ignore her bleating and force her to dance to the song. And depending on my level of annoyance, I'd let the song play a few minutes longer than usual. Most dancers would begrudgingly dance through to the end and then rush to the DJ booth afterwards for an explanation of the grave offense. Apologetically, I'd tell them that I couldn't read their writing or forgot to write the song down. It was in my best interest to placate them, as they were tipping me. At the Ruby Club, I devised a system where I would write the dancer's music and lighting preferences on index cards. I'd write the song titles that she had requested in the past and reference the card before she went onstage. This way I always knew what music she preferred and would invariably play her a great set, which ensured me a good tip at the end of the night. I never shared these cards with the other DJs and would lock them up with my equipment at the end of my shift. While it amused me that most of the dancers thought I had some mutant-like musical sensibility through which I intrinsically knew all of their favorite songs, it was obvious that they were too drunk or high to realize that I wrote the song titles on index cards. They'd remark that the best thing about working on my shifts was that "I always know what to play for them, and they don't even have to ask me for a song." They fully trusted me with their music selection. I'm probably the only strip club DJ who actually took notes on strippers. Most DJs couldn't care less. It worked out well for me, and I made a lot of money from those index cards.

If the dancer tipped well, I would usually play her any song that she requested, well, within reason. Most don't care what the DJ plays or are simply too high to be bothered to pick out their music. It's the new dancers that are problematic. The Ruby Club had several hundred girls on their roster. There were new girls almost every shift, which kept the job interesting but also incredibly irritating for the DJ. When I first started working night shifts, I grew accustomed to encountering novice dancers and created an elaborate introductory routine where I'd call the new dancers to the DJ booth, introduce myself, and inquire about her musical preference. That way, it appeared as if I actually gave a semblance of a fuck. These initial encounters were almost always frustrating and extremely annoying. One Thursday we had several new dancers start that night shift, and I called them all—over the microphone—to the booth to check in with me. After about ten minutes, only one dancer actually showed up with less than two minutes left before she had to go onstage.

"Hello, darling. My name's Dave. How are you? You're new, right?" I extended my hand, but the lithe, blonde dancer merely looked at it with the puzzled expression of someone completely ignorant of the custom. Perhaps she was foreign. Most upscale strip clubs have a diverse assortment of dancers from around the world. I'd say it's one of the more culturally varied environments I've ever worked in. After a few seconds of staring at my hand, she gingerly shook it, and nodded rather than answer my question. I noticed that she was a thin girl—not much older than twenty-two—with large, pendulous breasts that appeared authentic but were most likely artificial. Nevertheless, I'm always impressed by a top-notch breast augmentation.

"What's your name?" I had to look up when I addressed her because in her seven-inch heels she was at least four inches taller than me.

"Brie."

"Like the cheese."

"No, not like the cheese."

"Okay. So, B-r-e-e."

"No, B-r-i-e."

"Yeah, like the cheese."

"No, what cheese? There's no cheese."

Apparently, she was unaware that Brie is a type of cheese. "All right. Brie-not-like-the-cheese. I'll remember that. So, you're going onstage next. What type of music do you like?" Brie stood fixedly and stared, doe-eyed and quizzical for several seconds, twirling a lock of her hair around her right index finger, before responding.

"I dunno. What do you have?"

Expecting this response and conscious of the rapidly depleting time, I remarked as politely as possible, "Well, I have about six books of CDs filled with music from just about every genre. What type of music do you like?"

164

Again, Brie greeted me with her thousand-yard stare and complete lack of comprehension. With her face staring down at her cellphone, she apathetically inquired, "Do you have that one song by that guy?"

"And what song would that be? I have a lot of songs by lots of guys." I'm struggling to maintain a polite demeanor.

"You know, that one? Everyone loves it," she replied, still staring down at her cellphone, not even bothering to make eye contact. I felt like her tenth grade Geometry teacher.

"Is it a rock song or a rap song? Do you know the chorus or the name? Do you know anything about this song at all?" At this point, my patience was wearing thin.

Brie stood there utterly perplexed. Cogitating my difficult query for a few moments, she looked up at me with her inherent vacuous expression and said, "I dunno. I don't care. Just play something dancy."

Just play something dancy, she said. Play something dancy. I still sigh when I hear this phrase. In fact, I'm sighing as I write it. I sigh because the words feel like heartburn when I hear them slide between a stripper's glossy lips. I sigh because I realize that I've been slowly drowning in the shallow end of the intelligence gene pool for the past five years. Finally, I sigh because what the fuck is "play something dancy" supposed to mean? Seriously, what the fuck is that? I still have no idea. "Dancy" has to be the least descriptive term I have ever heard applied to music. I wouldn't even use the term to describe a type of dance music, like house or trance. All music could be considered "dancy" to some extent. The state of being "dancy" is purely idiosyncratic. What one might consider dancy might not be considered the least bit dancy to another. And I'm quite sure that what I consider to be dancy would not be accepted as dancy to any stripper that I've ever encountered.

Regrettably, we were at an impasse. I watched Brie indifferently texting away, her hot pink fingernails furiously clicking on the plastic buttons of her BlackBerry, and I realized that my life was an endless game of Chutes and Ladders, except the chutes and ladders in this game were covered in herpes. I still had not determined the type of music this girl preferred, and even worse she had about ten seconds left before she had to go onstage.

I was baffled and beyond the point of exasperation. "And what do you consider to be dancy?"

Before exiting the booth, she paused in the doorway, turned her head to face me, and with an expression that clearly registered her disdain for the pathetic whining dwarf of a man behind her, she replied, "I dunno. You're the DJ." And, with that, she flipped her head back around and sauntered down the hallway, pausing momentarily to adjust her neon pink thong.

She had a point there. I was the DJ. And in her mind, all DJs possessed a prescient ability to know exactly what music a girl considered to be dancy. I played her two popular house tracks from a Paul Oakenfold compilation. House music: innocuous, rhythmic, and played in clubs throughout the world. The music is so generic that it's invariably a safe bet. An hour later, in a drunken state, Brie stumbled to the DJ booth and while clinging to the doorway for balance she screamed, "Hey, DJ. You suck. That wasn't dancy."

I looked at the drunken girl leaning through the doorway and cracked a wry smile. "I suck, huh? Well, please tell me something more 'dancy' that you'd like to hear."

"I dunno. I'm not the DJ. You are. Just fucking pick something."

I really despised that woman. Don't get me wrong, I'd still have sex with her, but it would be a hateful, unforgiving rut, like the kind that occurs in the animal kingdom. For her next set, I chose two eighties songs: Dead or Alive's "You Spin Me Round" followed by Prince's "Kiss." You'd be hard-pressed to find a more "dancy" set than that. In my opinion, Prince songs define the neologism "dancy." Two hours passed before another unwelcome Brie appearance. She was completely inebriated at this point and could barely maintain her balance on those stilts she was wearing. I watched her precariously sway back and forth in her seven-inch stilettos, tightly clutching the doorframe with her right hand and her martini glass with her left. I didn't try to help her because, honestly, I wanted to see her fall. A new dancer tumbles at least once or twice every shift. It's an impressive feat to walk around in seven-inch heels stone sober, let alone after drinking martinis for the past three hours. Tumbling down a staircase and having a customer prematurely ejaculate on your thigh are rites of passage for new strippers. Brie stared at me for about a minute, her body leaning on the doorframe. She mumbled something, but she slurred so heavily that I couldn't make out what she was trying to say.

"Are you okay?" I asked, trying to sound concerned.

"You...You...S-s-s-uck," she stammered.

"Okay. Why do I suck?" I thought I'd try to reason with the intoxicated person. That's always entertaining.

She could barely hold herself up. "You j-j-ust s-suck."

"All right. I think you should probably head home. You seem pretty drunk."

Brie's martini glass slipped from her hand and crashed onto the floor, splashing vodka and vermouth across the wall. This made her laugh hysterically, and when she bent over to pick the glass up, she fell forward, face first, onto the ground. I rushed over to help the sprawled dancer.

"Damn. Are you all right?"

I attempted to help her stand up, but she pushed my hands away. "You suck. I hate old sh-i-i-i-t. Prince s-s-ucks."

I ignored her drunken blathering but was deeply offended. She deserved to be slapped for insulting Prince. "Let me help you stand up, and you can rest on that couch. And, for the record, Prince does not suck."

"Prince s-s-s-ucks!" she screamed and started laughing hysterically again. At this point, Brie had managed to roll over onto her ass, and with her legs in the air, she playfully kicked at me while still screaming, "Prince sucks!" over and over again.

"Stop that. You need to get off the floor." I jumped back before her right heel would have smashed into the side of my head.

"T-t-t-ake m-my heels off."

"Okay. Sit still and stop kicking me." Brie was still laughing but stopped kicking long enough for me to unbuckle her right shoe. She reached over and removed her left on her own. Grabbing Brie under her armpits, I hoisted her to her feet, surprised at how little she weighed. Without her heels on, she couldn't have been more than 5'3" and maybe weighed 105 pounds. I steered the drunken girl to the couch, and she collapsed onto it, pulling me on top of her.

She began kissing my neck while simultaneously apologizing for her obnoxious behavior. "I'm s-sorry. Y-y-you don't suck. I l-l-ike you. I'm s-s-sorry. I'm d-d-drunk."

"Really? I had no idea."

"Ha, ha. You're funny. You remind me of Dane Cook."

"Dane Cook? You are drunk and possibly retarded." I gently pushed her away and tried to stand up, but all in one motion, she grabbed my neck, pulled me on top of her, and shoved her tongue in my mouth. Her breath smelled like cigarettes and garlic. "Jesus, stop. Seriously. Stop!" I slipped out of her vise-like grip and backed away. Brie started giggling and lay on her back looking at me mischievously.

"What? You don't want these?" She pulled her bikini top to either side and freed her large D-cup breasts. She then pinched her nipples and cupped her breasts while playfully sliding her tiny pink tongue around her lips.

"Yes, of course. But I-I-I…" I was trying to rationalize the reason I was not licking her breasts at the moment. "I can't. I'm working. And if I get caught messing around with you, I'll be fired." At Ruby, there were only two major infractions a DJ could commit on the job: fucking a dancer, and snorting cocaine. If he's caught engaging in either of those activities, he'd be fired on the spot. Unfortunately, the potential for both was there almost every night. As difficult as it was for me to abstain, I did not want to be fired that night, especially on account of this drunken idiot. "Listen, I have to work. You can chill here if you want, but you gotta leave me alone."

"You're no fun," Brie pouted and lay back on the couch, not bothering to put her top back on.

I walked over to the console and checked to see how much time was left of the current song. There was over a minute, which was more than enough time to pick out music for the next dancer. Glancing at the whiteboard, I could see that Cinnamon was coming up next, and I knew that she liked hip-hop. I flipped through my book of CDs until I found Notorious BIG's "Hypnotize," one of her favorite songs, and cued it in the CD player. I announced Cinnamon to the stage and pressed play, before I felt a small hand slide down the back of my pants. Instantly, I whipped around and was met by a fully nude Brie standing directly behind me.

"Whoa, what the fuck are you doing? Where are your clothes?"

Brie giggled, grabbed my head on either side, and shoved my face between her breasts. I reared back but not before she pulled me towards her and forced her tongue in my mouth. Though her breath reeked, I was turned on and forcefully kissed her back. Still kissing her, I leaned over and slammed the door to the DJ booth shut. In one motion, I lifted her small frame onto the bar stool next to the console and shoved her back against the wall. I grabbed her massive breasts and began licking and biting her nipples but stopped short when Brie emitted a retching sound like a cat attempting to dislodge a hairball.

"Are you okay?" I asked, actually concerned this time.

"Come here…" She pressed her lips against mine and I shoved my tongue into her mouth, when, without warning, it happened. Brie burped and retched again before expelling a stream of puke into my mouth. I instinctively jerked away, but the vomit continued to shoot out of her mouth, leaving my face, neck, and chest covered in half-digested linguine noodles and chunks of clam and garlic. I began dry heaving as I pulled a piece of clam off my bottom lip and ran to the trash bin just in time to empty the contents of my stomach. When I finished, I looked up to see Brie crawling naked on all fours in a puddle of vomit. She was crying and laughing at the same time.

"What the fuck is wrong with you?"

"Wha—" Brie was laughing so hard that she couldn't even speak. Her hand suddenly slipped and she fell onto her left shoulder into the puddle of vomit. Now, her puke was all over her naked body, and her hair had so many pieces of garlic, clam, and partially digested bits of pasta that it looked like a blonde spiderweb dotted with the corpses of rotting insects. She rolled over onto her back, in the puddle of vomit, still crying and laughing hysterically.

"Jesus Christ. I can't fucking believe this. You need to clean yourself up and get out of here." I grabbed a roll of paper towels from the shelf and wiped her puke from my face and neck. Since my Calvin Klein black dress shirt was soiled, I undressed and put on an oversized Ruby Club white T-shirt. It didn't look as large once I tucked it into my pants.

"I'm going to call a house mom to come up here and help clean you up. This is fucking ridiculous."

"No, please d-don't." Brie looked up at me pleadingly. She wasn't laughing now. "I'm new. I'll get canned if they see me like this."

"Oh, fuck. I don't need this." I helped the naked girl to her feet and gave her some paper towels and water to clean herself off with. She ambled over to the couch and clumsily put on her bikini, which was untouched by the torrent of vomit. Laughing under my breath as she picked chunks of food out of her hair, I returned to the console and noticed that Cinnamon had been onstage for almost two full songs.

"Hey, do you have a cigarette?" Brie asked, still picking out bits of food from her hair.

171

"I only have one left. I'm sure someone in the dressing room has an extra smoke."

"I can't go down there right now. Can I split it with you?"

"Here, don't smoke the whole thing." After this experience, I needed a cigarette. More like, I needed a shower and some morphine. I took Cinnamon off the stage, announced the next dancer, and put on a house compilation. Thankfully, there were only two dancers left. I really needed this night to end. "Hey, let me have a hit."

"Oh, no. You shouldn't. I have a nasty cold sore." Brie didn't even bother to make eye contact, her attention was focused on her cellphone. It might have been the fact that we had just sucked eachother's faces and she neglected to mention this or maybe her blasé response, but either way, I was done dealing with this girl.

"That's it. Out. Now. Go!" I threw open the door and stared daggers at the blonde idiot smoking my last cigarette on the couch.

"Damn. Why are you tripping?"

"Out. Out. Out," I yelled pointing at the doorway.

"Okay, okay. Calm down. Geez." Brie smashed out the cigarette in her martini glass, picked up her purse, and sauntered past me. She stopped briefly just outside the door and turned her head around to face me. "And, for your information, those songs you played weren't dancy."

It took every ounce of restraint for me to resist punching her in the face, but instead, I smiled widely and waved goodbye with my middle finger. Sadly, these "play something dancy" experiences occurred once a night at almost every club I've worked at. I was in my own living hell, but at least I was being paid good money to be there. Eventually, I ceased asking the new girls what type of music they liked altogether. I didn't care anymore. If they didn't specifically tell me beforehand, then they were dancing to either rock or house, depending on the crowd or my mood at the time.

Mariah Carey's Rainbow

As I mentioned before, music selection varied based on the quality of the club and the clientele the club attracted. At most upscale clubs, the DJ controls the music, and other than suggesting songs that they like, the dancers have little input in music selection. Conversely, at the lower-tier clubs like the Doll House or Foxys, the dancers were allowed to bring in their own music and would meet with the DJ before their stage show to select the songs that they planned to dance to. I never understood the reason management allowed them to do that. Every dancer seemed to own one of these nondescript black CD books containing about thirty discs shoved haphazardly inside. I think they purposely bought the same cases and refused to mark them with their names just to annoy the DJs. We called them to the DJ booth to "check sound" prior to their stage show so they could pick out the music for their set.

"Gentlemen, round number two with sexy Coco. Destiny will be up next. Destiny, check sound."

When they heard their name being called, they'd run to the booth with a minute left before they had to go onstage and, in a shrill, panicked voice, ask for their CD case. I'd look at the shelf behind me that held about forty of these nondescript black CD books, and then look back at the girl with a frown.

"And which case is yours?"

To my chagrin, she'd apathetically respond while staring blankly at her cellphone, "The black one."

Yes, of course, the black one. Less than thirty seconds remaining, I'd have to rummage through all forty of the CD cases, find hers, and then allow her to pick out her music. And to make matters worse, the tardy dancer would have the temerity to ask me to cue her song in an unused CD player so that she can listen to it and determine whether it's the song she wants. Resisting the urge to verbally eviscerate her, I'd try to explain as diplomatically as possible that we didn't have enough time to do that.

"Baby, we're running out of time, just play what you did last set. Okay?"

"All right. But I wanna dance to something else next time."

"No problem. Just come over here five minutes before you go on, and we'll pick something out."

I said this to placate her, even though we both knew that she'd forget this conversation as soon as she exited the booth and an hour later we'd repeat this same scenario. Working at a strip club is a lot like the movie *Groundhog Day* but with tits. It was a mystery to me why the dancers didn't just write their names or put a butterfly, dolphin, or fairy—they obviously liked these symbols because most had them tattooed on their lower backs—or some other type of marking on their cases. This would not only ease the entire music selection process, but it would also aid the DJ in returning her CD to the proper case. And this was a lesson I learned the hard way: Never lose a dancer's CD. Let me amend this by adding: Never scratch a dancer's CD either. A dancer will never again tip a DJ if he loses or damages one of her CDs. She will hate him for eternity. Any occasion that his name enters into conversation

176

with other DJs, dancers, or management, she will refer to him as the "asshole" that lost her CD. Despite his explanations or even reparations, she'll never forgive him for this transgression. Never. In her small, myopic mind, he will be forever branded an asshole. And worst-case scenario, she'll convince her friends to hate him and not to tip him either. Just don't lose the dancers' CDs. Protect them like you would an adorable puppy.

At the Doll House, I worked with a soulless harpy named Selena. I'd be willing to wager that there is a Hispanic stripper at every club across the country that uses the stage name Selena. This particular Selena was an eighteen-year-old Latina who was very specific about her music selection. To the extent of being considered obsessive-compulsive, she meticulously labeled each CD with her name—both fake and real—and her tracks of choice. Amazingly, she was one of those rare dancers who even labeled her CD case with her name. But there was no mistaking Selena's CD case as it was emblazoned with stickers bearing the Rocawear insignia. Working in the strip club industry led me to the observation that this fashion line is extremely popular amongst young Latinas. Selena was completely outfitted in Rocawear clothing. From headband and jumpsuit to belt buckle and pom-pom socks, she was a walking advertisement for Jay-Z's clothing line. It should come as no surprise that her case was filled with rap and R&B music, and of her entire collection, I'd have to say that her favorite CD was Mariah Carey's late nineties album *Rainbow*. She coveted this god-forsaken record and danced to two tracks off it every time she went onstage. I heard those wretched songs so many times that I subconsciously memorized the lyrics. To this day, if I walked into a club and heard any track off the Mariah Carey *Rainbow* album, I'm sure I could sing it. If not the entire song, then at least the chorus.

Now, I was well aware of the precise organization of Selena's CD case and took great measures to carefully put the *Rainbow* CD in its demarcated plastic sleeve. Most strippers hardly know what day it is, let alone the condition of their CD case, so it was highly unusual to encounter such organization from one. And since Selena was a decent tipper, I went out of my way to look after her CDs. I sincerely appreciated how much she cared for her music, mostly because it was the only thing we had in common. One harried Friday evening at the Doll House, I played the Mariah Carey *Rainbow* set for Selena, and when the second song came to an end, I pressed the eject button on the CD player to retrieve her disc—but nothing happened. It would not eject the CD. I pressed the button again, and it still would not eject. I was confounded. The three other CD trays were working fine, but for some reason, tray four would not open. This had happened to me once or twice before with the ancient CD players at that club, but after hitting the eject button a few times eventually the tray would slide out. Trying not to panic, I pounded the eject button five or six times but to no avail. It would not open. My next recourse was to force it open with my Swiss Army knife. I jimmied the longer blade under the tray and tried to slowly pry it open. I had to be careful because management would have a conniption if I damaged their precious equipment. God forbid they might have to replace these twenty-year-old pieces of shit. Finally, the tray slid open, but surprisingly, the Mariah Carey *Rainbow* CD wasn't on it. The disc was nowhere to be found. I grabbed a flashlight and searched under, around, and above the CD player. Frantically, I looked through all of the girls' cases just in case I placed it in the wrong one. But despite my thorough search, I couldn't find it. It seemed to have vanished into thin air. My only conclusion was that the CD player had swallowed the disc and it was stuck somewhere inside the machine. There was no other explanation. Knowing that Selena would scrutinize her case at the end of the night and discover the missing *Rainbow* CD, I had no choice but to explain to her that the machine had swallowed the disc and I was unable to retrieve it. Anyone that meticulous had to be a rational person and should understand that these things happen at low-end strip clubs that use faulty machinery. Besides, she earned more than enough money in one night shift to buy twenty copies of that record. The shift ended about an hour later, and when Selena arrived at the booth to collect her CD book, I calmly informed her of the situation.

"Hey, Selena, I'm sorry to have to say this, but the CD player swallowed your Mariah Carey disc. It won't come out of the machine. This is a total piece of shit." I pointed to the machine and shook my head, trying to look as apologetic as possible even though I was somewhat relieved that I wouldn't have to hear those horrid songs any more.

Selena flashed me an incredulous look and pondered what I had just said for a few seconds before replying with a laconic, "Huh?" I calmly explained the situation to her a second time. The news finally registered. And when it did, she snarled her lips and, with her thick hood rat inflection, said, "Bitch, you gots me heated. I best be getting my Mariah right fuckin' now!" She cocked her head back and jerked it from side to side as she spoke, and her right hand bitch-slapped the air in front of my face.

Her response caught me off guard. Up until this point in my life, I don't think I had ever been called a "bitch" by a woman, and

179

furthermore, I was confused as to what she wanted me to do. I wasn't about to dismantle the machine and retrieve the CD for her. And I didn't own *Rainbow*, so I couldn't give her my copy.

"Selena, look, I'm sorry. The machine ate your disc and I can't get it out. You should ask Joe to replace it for you."

"Fuck that shit. Give me my motherfuckin' Mariah. You stole it, bitch. I want it back."

"Do you honestly believe that I stole your Mariah Carey CD?"

With her lips still snarled, she replied, "Yeah. Where's it at? Give it back, bitch."

This time she said the word "bitch" rather loudly and alerted the other dancers who were lining up to cash out their money with the manager. Now all eyes were focused on the altercation in the DJ booth. At this point, my patience had worn thin.

"Okay. First, I'm not a fucking bitch. My name's Dave. Second, look at me. Do I look like a person who listens to Mariah Fucking Carey? Seriously, do I? No. I don't. Look through my CD case: Metallica, Motorhead, Motley Crue. No Fucking Mariah Carey. I don't have your fucking CD. I'm sorry, but your CD is in this piece-of-shit machine, and I can't do anything about that. All right?"

Now, we had the undivided attention of everyone in the room, including the General Manager, Joe, who was marching towards the DJ booth to see what was going on. Selena's face was red, and it appeared as if she was trembling a bit. Those weren't fear trembles. Those were anger trembles. She looked at me and menacingly waved her index finger and thumb of her right hand in a gun sign towards me.

"Shut the fuck up, nigga. My man finna bust a cap in yo grill. Give me my Mariah now. He'll be bustin caps up in this bitch."

She then snatched her cellphone out of her pink leather Rocawear bag and began hysterically pushing numbers. Frankly, her last statement alarmed me. I had picked up some hood slang since I had been at the club, and I was well aware that the terms "grill" and "cap busting" being used together in this fashion did not bode well for me. But even though I was clearly being threatened, the ridiculous notion that I might be shot in the face because of a Mariah Carey CD made me smile. I lit a cigarette, sat down, and let her continue on with her rant. She was screaming at me and in her phone simultaneously. Struggling to maintain composure, I broke into a fit of laughter. Some of the other dancers noticed me laughing, which subsequently made them laugh. This aggravated the situation and made Selena furious. Now, she was screaming not only at me but at the other dancers as well, which caused one of them to confront her. A large black girl named Chantel knocked her phone out of her hand and faced off with her. I thought for sure there was going to be a girl fight. It was like a scene from some USA Network B-Movie, *Psycho Prison Sluts from Cellblock 20*. By this time, Joe stepped in between the two girls and yelled louder than both of them combined.

"Shut the fuck up! Now! What the fuck is wrong with you?"

Joe demanded to know what had happened and glared at Selena. He had this power to terrify women, which is most likely the reason he spent several years in prison for domestic abuse. Nevertheless, it's a good skill to have for a strip club manager. Selena pointed at me and started blabbering an incomprehensible version of the story. Unable to understand a word she was saying, Joe heatedly looked at me and demanded to know what had happened.

"What the fuck is going on over here, Sanchez?"

"Joe, the CD player ate her Mariah Carey CD. I tried to get it out, but it's stuck in there. I attempted to explain this to her, but she won't listen. She thinks I took it."

I could see the rage forming in his eyes. Joe had an irascible nature, and when provoked, he didn't calm easily. He paused for a moment to evaluate my testimony, like a judge would a defendant, before focusing the brunt of his anger on Selena, the plaintiff.

"What the fuck is wrong with you? Listen. The machine ate your fucking CD. The DJ didn't take it. What? Are you stupid? Look at me when I'm talking to you. If you can't get along with the DJ or the girls in this club, you can get the fuck out right fucking now! And if I ever hear you threaten one of my employees, I'll call the police and have your fat ass arrested. Now get the fuck out of my face!"

Joe's outburst brought an abrupt end to the altercation. Fighting back tears, Selena cashed out, glowered a couple of times in my direction, and hastily left the club. I felt like I should have thanked Chantel for defending my honor, but I didn't end up saying anything to her. I doubt she was fighting for me. It seemed more plausible that she had some personal grudge against Selena and this was as good a time as any to settle it.

The following Sunday, before my shift started, I stepped outside the club to smoke a cigarette and noticed Selena sitting in the back of a purple car parked across the street, smoking a joint with two men. I was surprised that someone would smoke a joint in such an absurdly conspicuous vehicle. The car was a purple 1980s Chevrolet Caprice that was perched on top of four tires with grossly disproportionate chrome rims. The rims had such a large diameter that the entire vehicle was raised almost three feet off the ground. But that wasn't the absurd part. The absurd part was the airbrushed painting on the driver's side door of Grimace—the purple McDonalds character—wearing a Kangol hat, a thick gold chain, and making gang symbols with his hands. Of all the McDonaldland characters to be misappropriated by "urban" culture, you'd think Grimace would have been towards the bottom just above the annoying bird girl. Now that I think about it, it seems like it would be much more fitting to choose The Hamburglar, as he seems like he would have more "street cred" than Grimace.

Once Selena spotted me smoking, she nudged the driver and pointed her finger out the window at me. Trying not to appear intimidated, I calmly finished my cigarette and pretended not to notice them. Around 10:00 PM, I took my break and saw that the purple Caprice was still parked across the street. The windows were rolled up and tinted dark black, which made it a bit difficult to tell if there was anyone inside, but I could hear loud rap music blaring from the vehicle. I chose to ignore the car completely and decided to walk to one of the pizza restaurants up the street and get a slice.

As soon as I started walking, the Caprice roared to life, whipped out of its parking spot, pulled a U-turn across Broadway Avenue, and slowly crept behind me. The bass from the car's subwoofers boomed so loudly that it rattled the car's chassis, creating an obnoxious rattling sound that set off the alarms of several parked cars. For a Sunday night, the streets were desolate. I didn't even see any drunken tourists milling about. Now I was beginning to get nervous, and at that moment, I found it much less humorous that I might get shot because of a Mariah Carey record. They tailed me for two blocks to the restaurant, parked on the corner, and watched me walk inside. I briefly considered asking the cashier if I could borrow his phone and call 911, but nothing had happened to me. Yet. Would these guys really "bust a cap" in me for something so insignificant? Why would they risk life in prison for something so trivial as a Mariah Carey record? And a mediocre record at that. I felt thick beads of perspiration slide down my forehead when it dawned on me that these are the type of people who murder other people for their shoes. I'm fucked. I tried to soothe my anxiety with a couple of bites of my greasy slice of mushroom and cheese pizza, but my appetite had vanished. I quickly glanced over my shoulder to see if the car was still parked outside. It was still there. And to make matters worse, my fifteen-minute break was quickly coming to an end. My options were limited to calling the police, ordering more food and hiding out in the restaurant, or returning to work. I reluctantly chose the third option, took a deep breath—not sure if it would be my last—and timidly pushed the glass door open. I shoved a cigarette in my mouth and turned to walk back towards the club when I noticed the tinted passenger side window of the Caprice roll down. This was it. I'm about to be shot on a sidewalk in North Beach. I braced myself for the salvo of bullets, but none came. Instead, the window rolled down to reveal the chubby face of a young black man in his mid-twenties wearing a black Oakland Raiders hat, dark sunglasses, and a Raiders football jersey over a white T-shirt. He was smoking a massive blunt, and as I walked by his window, he removed the blunt from his mouth and slowly exhaled a thick grey plume of pungent marijuana smoke and laughed. His teeth were capped in gold. Though I couldn't make out the face of the driver, I could hear him laughing in the background as well. My heart was beating so fast that I felt I might be having a heart attack. I practically ran back to the club and only stopped to catch my breath once I was safely in the DJ booth.

My shift ended a few hours later, and I waited for Casey to leave with me so we could share a cab back to the Tenderloin. When we left the club and walked up Broadway, I saw that the purple Caprice was still parked there, waiting for me. Perhaps it was out of hubris or fear that he'd confront them, but I chose not to mention anything about the incident to Casey. We caught a cab, and ten minutes later, I was home safe in my studio apartment. I lay back in bed and was about to turn on the TV when I heard the ominous bass-filled boom of rap music coming from outside. No way. There was no way they could have found out where I lived. I jumped out of bed, shut off the light, and cautiously lifted up the window blinds, only slightly, so I could peer out onto the street below. And sure enough, there was the purple Caprice parked on the street in front of my building. Pangs of fear shot through my gut like spoiled Mexican food. They know where I live. How? Did they follow the cab, or did someone give them my address? It didn't matter because they were outside right now. Not wanting to draw any attention to myself, I carefully lowered the blinds and slowly stepped backwards away from the window. I climbed back into bed and pulled the covers up high and lay there listening to the boom of the bass blasting through the night. If their goal was to scare the shit out of me, they had certainly achieved it.

I didn't have to work the next two days but didn't leave my apartment. Every so often, I'd sneak a quick peek out my window to see if the purple Caprice was still parked outside. It was still there. They hadn't left. They were waiting for me to walk outside. And then what? A severe thrashing? A bullet to the chest? Soon it was Wednesday and I had to work that night. Maybe I could slip out the back of the building and hop in a cab, but then they'd just follow me to work or be waiting for me when I return. I could call the police and have them sort this out, but I really didn't want to do that. I didn't trust the police any more than the gangbangers. I had no other choice but to confront them and find out what they wanted. I refused to be held hostage in my own apartment, especially by two guys driving a Grimacemobile. It took about a pint of whiskey and a series of deep breathing exercises to summon the courage to walk outside my building and approach the purple car. I stood next to the driver's window for a full minute before it slowly rolled down, allowing a thick cloud of marijuana smoke to escape from the cabin. The driver was a well-built black man who couldn't have been any older than twenty-five. He had a shaved head and wore dark sunglasses and a gold chain with a Raiders helmet pendant hanging in the middle of his broad chest. His face looked very familiar. I must have seen him waiting for Selena outside of the club. His heavyset companion with the gold teeth sat in the passenger seat, and both men stared out the driver's window at me, stunned to see me standing there.

"Excuse me, fellas. Do I know you? H-h-have I met you bef—"

The driver answered before I was finished. "Yo, you work wit' my girl and you gaffled her shit." He had taken a drag off a blunt before he spoke, and small plumes of smoke slid from his lips with every word.

"Oh, okay. You must be friends of Selena. Umm. Actually, I didn't gaffle her shit. What happened was—"

He cut me off again. "Yo, I ain't here to listen to yo bullshit. I came to get my girl's Mariah CD."

"Okay, that's the conundrum. I don't have her CD. I think it's stuck in one of the shitty CD players at the club."

When I said this, his friend in the passenger seat spoke up, "Fuck this. Teach this nigga a lesson, Rome."

I could feel this parley taking a turn for the worse and had to think of something fast.

"You don't have to teach me a lesson. I feel horrible about this whole situation. Selena is a wonderful person and one of my favorite dancers. You know what? I'm going to buy her a new Mariah Carey *Rainbow* CD right now."

Rome, the driver, took a hit off his blunt and looked me at me for a few seconds before muttering, "Damn right you finna buy that shit."

"Hey, since you guys have a car, would you mind giving me a lift to Tower Records? It's just up Market."

"Hell no," Rome said as both he and his passenger erupted into laughter. "This white boy's trippin'."

"Hey, a guy at work gave me a blunt filled with the chronic. You guys can totally have it if you give me a ride."

The hefty companion glanced at me and then shifted his attention to Rome. "Chronic? Yo, Rome, we ain't got much left. Let's give this nigga a ride."

I didn't wait for a response. "Great. Let me run upstairs and grab the blunt. Are you fellas hungry? I have Doritos."

Rome gave me a slightly annoyed look and shook his head, but his friend seemed excited. "Yeah, bring that shit. You got any beer?"

"I think so." I headed back to my apartment and returned a few minutes later with a massive blunt, a bag of Nacho Cheese Doritos, and a six-pack of Corona. I climbed into the backseat of the car trying not to crush the empty fast-food bags lining the floor. The exterior of the vehicle was far better maintained than the interior, but to be fair, these guys had been camping out in front of my apartment for a couple days and didn't have much time to clean. The seats were covered with black leather upholstery, which matched the dark interior of the car, and as I sat down, I noticed that the vehicle's suspension was modified so that the front end was raised slightly higher than the rear, causing me to slide back into the leather seat. This car really was ridiculous.

"Hey, thanks for giving me a ride. My name's Dave but everyone at the club calls me Sanchez." I reached out my hand, but neither of them bothered to take it.

"I'm Omar and this big nigga over here's Rome," said the heavyset guy in the passenger seat, straining to turn around and face me.

"Nice to meet you. This is a great ride. What do you call this? A hooptie?"

"Hooptie? This nigga said hooptie! Nah. This shit's a motherfuckin' box!" Omar seemed somewhat offended by my question.

"My apologies. I didn't know. Well, you have a nice box." I handed both Rome and Omar a Corona and sparked the blunt. When Rome started the car, the engine was so loud that it startled me and I almost dropped the lit joint onto the floor. Luckily, I caught it before it ignited the piles of discarded fast-food bags. I took another hit and passed the blunt to Omar.

He took a long hit, smiled, and nodded. "Good shit."

Rome took a couple hits, but it was mainly Omar and I who passed the blunt back and forth.

"So, I mean no offense by this, but what the fuck is Grimace supposed to be?" I asked.

"What?" Rome asked as Omar burst into laughter.

"You have a picture of Grimace on your car, and I'm wondering what the fuck he's supposed to be? A big, retarded gumdrop? A monster? What is he?"

"I thought he's a grape milkshake or summin," Omar answered as he took another long hit of the blunt and passed it back to me.

"No, he's definitely not a milkshake. McDonalds doesn't even have a grape milkshake. All of the other McDonalds characters make sense. You know. The fry guys are French fries. Mayor McCheese is obviously a cheeseburger. The bird chick is supposed to be a McNugget or a McChicken sandwich. But what the fuck is Grimace? He has no relation to a McDonalds' entrée."

"I dunno. I thought he was a milkshake wit' arms and legs," Omar answered.

"You both got it wrong. Grimace is an anthropomorphized tastebud," said Rome.

"Really? An anthropomorphized tastebud. How would you know that?" I don't know what surprised me more: the idea of Grimace being a tastebud, or Rome's use of the word "anthropomorphized."

"For real. That's what he is. I worked at McDonalds for three years, and this old dude who worked there schooled me about Grimace. He said Grimace started out as an evil motherfucker, stealing Ronald's milkshakes and shit. Back then, he was a tastebud with four arms. He was O.G., but then they made him into a good guy and gave him two arms. Now, he's kind of a retarded purple tastebud that chills with Ronald."

Omar took a hit off the blunt and burst into a fit of laughter and coughing. "This nigga said retarded purple tastebud."

"That's what he is, nigga. A tastebud. Look that shit up if you don't believe me."

"Really? I had no idea. I suppose I never gave it much thought," I responded, sounding somewhat impressed.

"Tastebud, huh? Damn. I thought that nigga was a milkshake," said Omar.

We continued driving up Market in silence, each of us contemplating how this revelation had forever altered our perceptions of the purple simpleton. Our reverie was broken a few minutes later by Omar.

"Where those Doritos at?"

"Here," I said, tossing the bag into the front seat.

We soon arrived at Tower Records, and I leaned forward to say goodbye. "Hey, thanks for the ride, man. I appreciate it. I'll buy your girl the Mariah CD."

Omar turned around to face me and shook my hand. "You better get that girl some Mariah cuz this nigga over here ain't had no pussy in a week."

"Shut the fuck up, nigga!" Rome replied angrily and raised his fist as if he was going to punch Omar in the face.

"Well, thanks again for the ride." I exited the car and stood on the sidewalk, watching it glide into traffic. That was probably the first and only time I will ever ride in a "box."

Honestly, I did feel remorse about this whole situation. It's an unspoken rule that the DJ must assume full responsibility for a dancer's CDs during his shift. While it was the fault of the club's equipment, I still felt personally responsible for the whole fracas. I had to make amends. And I did. I even endured the ridicule of the snarky Tower Records store employees to purchase that CD. Believe me, it's a very self-effacing experience for a man in his early thirties to approach the counter at a record store and ask for a copy of a Mariah Carey album. I attempted to explain the situation, but the heartless bastard just smiled and reassured me that Mariah Carey had many male supporters. He then asked a couple of other employees to help him lead me to the Mariah Carey section. Not even masking their puerile inside jokes, they told me that I would find many other fine Mariah Carey records in this section to add to my collection. I really wanted to beat them, but I was so stoned that I didn't care. Regardless, I bought the CD for Selena and gave it to her with a sincere apology. She didn't even have the courtesy to thank me. She merely smirked, grabbed the CD from my hand, and sauntered away from the booth muttering something about how fortunate I was that I didn't get "capped" by her man. My actions might have been unappreciated, but at least my conscience was clean. Six months later, the club's CD player officially stopped working and had to be replaced. When they moved it, Mariah Carey's *Rainbow* CD fell onto the ground along with about five or six other discs. Joe was working that night and made sure to save it for me. He ceremoniously presented it to me at the end of my next shift amidst a round of applause from my co-workers and several dancers. I still have it in my personal collection, as it's somewhat of a keepsake now.

Run to the Hills

Before I started working at a strip club, I naively assumed that all strippers danced to Motley Crue, Guns N' Roses, ACDC, or some other type of hair metal or butt rock. All of those bands had strippers in their videos, so it made perfect sense to me. Within my first week at the Doll House, I realized that I was sorely mistaken. Strippers might have danced to Motley Crue in the late eighties or early nineties, and occasionally you may walk into a strip club and see a girl dancing to a Poison song because her middle-aged regular requested it, but these days, the vast majority prefer to dance to hip-hop, rap, and in my opinion, one of the worst music genres of all, contemporary R&B.

Now, I consider myself to have a relatively diverse taste in music. As a vinyl enthusiast with several thousand records in my collection, my taste runs the gamut from The Misfits to Tupac. But I have a difficult time accepting contemporary R&B as a listenable music genre. It's almost worse than modern country music, which is, inarguably, the Special Olympics of music. For me, both are a slow and painful listening experience. I'd prefer to listen to *A Night at the Roxbury* soundtrack in its entirety followed by Nickelback's *Greatest Hits* than be subjected to a half hour of consecutive contemporary R&B songs. I make use of the term "contemporary R&B" in an effort to distinguish it from the R&B of the fifties, sixties, and seventies. James Brown, Al Green, Curtis Mayfield, Marvin Gaye, and The Isley Brothers are all classified within the R&B/Soul genre and are amazing artists deserving of utmost respect. I'm sure they were dismayed to see their musical creation evolve into a base, lurid form of adolescent sexual expression. It has become the mating soundtrack for the dim-witted and linguistically challenged. James Brown and Al Green would never have used these song titles: "Feelin' On Your Booty," "U Remind Me of My Jeep," "Knockin' Da Boots," "Freakin' You," "Shorty (Got Her Eyes on Me)," "I Can Tell U Wanna Fuck," or my personal favorite, "T-Shirt and Panties." I had never encountered the contemporary R&B genre prior to working at the Doll House. The names Jodeci, R. Kelly, and H-Town were foreign concepts to me. But within that first week of employment, I realized that contemporary R&B is the preferred music of the modern-day stripper. They like it—believe me, I've inquired—because it makes them feel "sexy" or the more common explanation, "I'm feeling tired and R&B is easy music to dance to." The latter is the primary reason they prefer R&B because they can roll about on their backs onstage and earn the same amount in tips as the dancer frenetically wrapping her body around the pole to Aerosmith's "Rag Doll."

The first several months at the Doll House was a veritable culture shock for me. I had several books of CDs at my disposal, but not one contained an R. Kelly song. I not only had to pay close attention to the music selection of the night shift DJs, I had to assiduously write down the music that the girls requested, or I would not have been a successful DJ at that club. It took about a month of studying this wretched genre and several weeks of downloading songs from the Internet before I had a decent collection of contemporary R&B music. On a daily basis, I'd pore through the Top 20 lists of all the urban radio stations and download the most popular tracks. Soon enough, I was able to play almost any song that a dancer requested, and they tipped me well for it.

That being said, if the dancer was a poor tipper, I couldn't care less what type of music she requested. I'd select music for the crowd and for myself. And more often than not, it would be some type of rock or metal because that's what I wanted to hear: ACDC, Aerosmith, Nine Inch Nails, Iron Maiden, Guns N' Roses, Motley Crue, Danzig, Alice in Chains, Metallica, The Stooges, or even Slayer or Motorhead if I really didn't like the girl. Experience has taught me that Slayer is a very effective tool in teaching a dancer the benefits of tipping the DJ. It's difficult to describe the sweeping feeling of satisfaction I derived from watching a dancer who refused to tip stand helplessly onstage, with a look of pure and intense hatred on her face while Slayer's "Angel of Death" blasted through the club's speakers. All strip club DJs live for these "fucking with the dancer moments," and we all have our anecdotes about how we played some outlandish song for a dancer we didn't like and she flipped out. I worked with a DJ who told me how he once played "Turning Japanese" followed by "Kung Fu Fighting" for an Asian dancer who never tipped him. She flashed him a nasty look during the first song and furiously exited the stage during the second. With her exposed mammoth fake breasts bouncing from left to right, she headed directly to the DJ booth and spat in his face while cursing at him in Cantonese. We all have a cache of novelty songs reserved for the non-tippers. Donnie, who I worked with at the Ruby Club, always employed MC Hammer's "U Can't Touch This" for non-tipping dancers. Now I've played "Baby Got Back" and "Ice Ice Baby" a few times, but I've never played MC Hammer for a dancer. Not once. I'm not that much of a sadist. But like any experienced strip club DJ, I had my special cache of songs that I reserved for the non-tippers.

At the end of my shift, I'd head downstairs while the girls cashed out with the managers and wait by the front door to make it as awkward as possible for them to leave without tipping me. Most of the seasoned dancers would tip or explain that they didn't make enough money that night and would take care of me the next time we worked together. I was satisfied with that explanation. Though it would have been better to receive some amount of compensation, it was also advantageous to remain on a dancer's good side. And when they did earn a lot of money, they'd usually tip me double that night. But there were always a few strippers who were either new and did not know that it was customary to tip the DJ and security staff, or ones that steadfastly refused to tip anything at all. I typically worked with a dancer for at least two or three shifts before I classified her as a non-tipper and played Weird Al for her sets. After the second shift when I didn't receive a tip, I'd confront her in a tactful manner and inquire as to why she chose not to tip. I'd like to emphasize being "tactful" in these interactions because, though it's customary, a dancer is not required to tip any employee at a strip club. And if she feels like she's being extorted or threatened in any manner, she could complain to management, and the DJ or bouncer would be immediately fired. It was much easier to replace a security guard or DJ than find an attractive dancer who was reliable and a good earner. When I was promoted to night shifts at the Doll House, I replaced an egotistical, violence-prone DJ named Terrence who would confront non-tipping girls in the most untactful manner possible. Terrence, or 'Tito' as everyone called him, was in his late twenties and became friends with my manager Joe when they were both in prison. Tito also waited by the front door to be tipped, but if a girl tried to leave without tipping, he'd grab her by the arm and corner her outside, demanding to know why she wasn't "breaking him off." He'd refer to this as his "gorilla pimp technique," and he informed me several times that "fear is the only way these bitches learn." Understandably, he frightened a lot of dancers and was eventually let go because one of them complained about his technique. Conversely, I chose to use a much softer, more diplomatic approach. Standing by the door, I'd watch the non-tipper cash out with the manager, and as she was walking by me to exit the club, I'd say in a very non-confrontational tone:

"Hey, Nadine, do you have a minute?"

"Umm, yeah."

"I was just wondering if I screwed up your set. Did I play the wrong song or something?"

"Umm, no. I don't think so."

"Yeah, I thought I played the two songs that you requested. Usually, if I play a decent set, most girls take care of me at the end of the night. I'm just concerned I did something to upset you because I haven't received a tip tonight or the last time we worked together."

"Oh, I'm sorry. I'm new and didn't realize that we had to tip." Slightly embarrassed, she'd rummage through her purse and pull out a twenty-dollar bill. "Will this work?"

"Totally. Thanks a lot. I appreciate it, and let me know if there's any new music that you'd like to dance to."

This self-deprecating approach was very effective for the majority of cases but not all. I've worked with several dancers who simply refused to tip regardless of how many times I'd passive-aggressively inquire about the reason they chose not to take care of me at the end of the night. These were the dancers who I had reserved a cache of special songs for.

Compared to my colleagues, I was rather patient and more than willing to give a dancer several chances to make amends. But after three shifts without receiving a tip, I had no choice but to ridicule her onstage with music, my only weapon. My go-to song for this situation was "What Is Love," the first track from *A Night at the Roxbury* soundtrack. In fact, most of the songs from that soundtrack would work perfectly. I'd follow that with Tom Jones's "Sex Bomb" or sometimes "Maneater" by Hall & Oates. All three of those songs are fast-paced and easily meet the 120-beats-per-minute requirement set by the management. For her second set of the night, I'd make the switch to metal and play Iron Maiden's "Run to the Hills" as loud as I could followed by Danzig's "Mother," which was applicable because a good portion of the dancers were single mothers. At most clubs, the dancer is never allowed to leave the stage unless it's an extreme circumstance, like her water broke or she's in the throes of an epileptic fit. If she has a temper tantrum and storms off the stage because of the DJ's music selection, she will incur a sizable fine. Therefore, she has no choice but to dance to the music the DJ has selected for her. I could play the hapless dancer a seven minute Iron Maiden song, and she had to dance to it. And depending on how many occasions she "forgot" to tip me and which manager was working that night, I'd play that Iron Maiden song in its entirety. The dancer would feign enjoyment for the duration of the song, and as soon as it finished, she'd angrily storm off the stage and march directly to the DJ booth.

"What the fuck was that?"

"That's my way of saying thanks for not tipping me."

This comment would silence her momentarily, affording me an opportunity to continue by bluntly explaining: "Like you, I earn my living primarily from tips. If you take care of me at the end of the night, I will play you any song that you desire. But if you choose to stiff me, well then, you'll have to dance to the music that I want to hear. And I love Iron Maiden. I really do. They're one of my favorite bands."

She stands there mouth agape, her maroon-shadowed oval eyes in their characteristic vacuous stare, and offers a feeble explanation: "Oh my god. I'm so sorry. I totally forgot to tip you last night."

"Well, actually, you forgot to tip me the last three nights that we worked together."

"Oh, shit. My bad. My money sucked the last few nights and I just forgot to tip you." Reaching into her purse, she'd pull out two twenty-dollar bills. "Is this okay?"

"That works. What do you want me to play for your next set? And I promise I won't play any Maiden."

"Umm, I'm feeling like in a rock mood. Do you have any Nickelback?"

Trying not to audibly sigh, "Yes, I do. I'll play some Nickelback for your next set." Say what you will about their wretched music, at least it's better than contemporary R&B.

After this brief conversation and a few sets of "non-tipper" music, most dancers would understand the benefits of tipping the DJ. However, there were invariably some who simply did not care and still refused to tip. The most resilient non-tipper that I ever encountered was a dancer named Barbie who worked at the Doll House for a brief period. She was a reasonably attractive blonde with some of the worst tattoos that I had ever seen. I shuddered every time I caught a glance of her My Little Pony tramp stamp. There were rumors that she was a Bulgarian model who had moved to America, fell on hard times, and consequently ended up at the Doll House. But none of these stories were ever substantiated. On more than one occasion, I had tried my self-deprecating inquisition but to no success. She'd glance apathetically in my direction and hastily walk out the front door with nary a thought of tipping me. But since she was new and easy on the eyes, I gave her five chances before I started fucking with her music. The other DJs at the club utterly despised her and had their worst music cued up as soon as she took the stage. After several weeks of not receiving a tip, I completely echoed their sentiment and played her some of the worst sets that I could muster. Barbie once worked one of my Friday day shifts, and only two other girls had shown up for work that day. This meant that she would have to go on the stage at least a dozen times. Casey was the manager for that shift, and he couldn't care less what I played for her. In fact, he stood in the DJ booth and offered suggestions:

"Have you played 'Mongoloid' yet?"

"No, I haven't played any Devo. This set is going to be all Journey."

I hit the play button and Journey's "Separate Ways" blasted from the club's speakers. Barbie didn't seem to pay any attention to the music. She took off her top and held onto the pole and circled it repeatedly, lacking any sort of rhythm to her movements. Without exaggeration, she was one of the most uncoordinated dancers that I had ever seen.

"Damn, Sanchez. I'd wager that you'd have more rhythm up there than she does."

"I've seen quadriplegics with more rhythm."

"Whatever. I couldn't care less about her. I'm just paying attention to the plight of Steve Perry. He's a man who loved and lost and may never have truly loved again," lamented Casey.

"What do you mean?"

"Listen to the song, man. Separate fucking ways. He had to go his separate way because he was bound by the chains of love. Stop talking and just fucking listen. He couldn't take those distant eyes anymore and he had to go his separate way. And I don't fucking blame him. We've all been there."

"Well, you've certainly been there. Steve might have been a tortured soul, but it sounds to me that he dated a lot of psychotic women. And didn't the keyboardist Jonathan Cain write this song?" I asked, knowing full well that the question would irritate Casey.

"What the fuck are you talking about? Steve wrote all the major hits for Journey. Sure, he might have collaborated with Cain and Schon on a few songs, but it was all Perry. These songs came from his soul. He was a lover. He gave so much and took so little. And these cunts threw it in his face. Fuck them. I'm with Steve on this."

I almost forgot that I was DJing, and without bothering to announce Barbie's second song, I faded into Journey's "Send Her My Love." She paid no attention and continued her uncoordinated, spastic dance routine around the pole. I looked over at Casey and noticed that he was pensively staring at the ceiling, his right hand gripping the bottom of his chin.

"You know, I've always found this song to be profoundly agonizing. It really affects the listener at his core," I said.

Casey ceased his rumination. "I know what you mean. Steve feels deep remorse for his actions. But his actions were inevitable. It's not like he never loved her. I mean, what'd you expect him to do? He's on the road so many nights a year. How could he adequately love a woman and raise a family with her? He tried, but ultimately, he had to let her go."

"You're right, man. He gave what he could, but he knew in his heart that it would never be enough. But he still cared."

"Yes, that he did." Casey sighed deeply, and we listened to the rest of the song in silence.

I would've continued to deconstruct Journey songs with Casey had I not looked at the soundboard and realized that Barbie had been dancing for almost ten minutes. I don't think she even noticed. In fact, I had to announce twice that it was time for her to leave the stage before she finally stepped down. Her next set consisted of Poison's "Unskinny Bop" followed by Night Ranger's "Sister Christian." Casey looked insulted by my choice for her second song.

"I'm shocked that you played this. I'm no prude, but a song about rape has no place in a strip club," he said accusingly.

"You're insane. 'Sister Christian' is about a young girl's coming of age."

"Pay attention to the lyrics for a second and you'll see that this song is about raping nuns."

We both watched Barbie clutch the pole tightly and move her hips in stark opposition to the tempo of the song. "That girl really has no sense of rhythm. I think she dances like that on purpose."

Casey ignored me and pointed his index finger in the air. "Listen to this part of the song." He looked over at me assuredly. "Her time has come? See, the nun clearly has no choice. Her time has come to be gang-raped by the sex-addicted members of Night Ranger. They're probably intoxicated or high on coke and think it's a good idea to rape a nun. It's hard for me to listen to this. Disgusting. Make it stop."

Though I thought he was reaching on this one, I faded the song out and put on the next dancer. For Barbie's next few sets, I emptied my cache of stripper torture music: Aerosmith's "Dude (Looks Like a Lady)" followed by The Butthole Surfers' "Lady Sniff"; WASP's

"Animal (Fuck Like a Beast)" and Neil Diamond's "Forever in Blue Jeans"; Slayer's "Kill Again" paired with Gwar's "I'm So Sick of You"; Cannibal Corpse's "Meat Hook Sodomy" and Warren Zevon's "Werewolves of London"; Willie D's "Bald Headed Hoes" followed by 2 Live Crew's "Face Down Ass Up." But it didn't bother her whatsoever. She paid no attention to the music I was playing and would walk off the stage without even glancing in the direction of the DJ booth. I was at wit's end. I had to unleash the nuclear bomb. The next set that I had chosen for Barbie would infuriate even the most tolerant of strippers. When she walked onstage for the final time that shift, I played my ultimate non-tipper set: Digital Underground's "The Humpty Dance" followed by Color Me Badd's "I Wanna Sex You Up." I have never met a stripper who didn't tip after being forced to dance to "The Humpty Dance" two or three times in a night. But, alas, my efforts fell flat. These songs didn't seem to faze her in the least bit. I was about to relent and accept the fact that I was never going to receive a tip from her, when a young Mexican dancer named Heaven approached the booth and asked:

"Why you playing all this wack shit for her? It won't do no good."

"What do you mean? These songs aren't wack."

"You trippin' if you think 'Humpty Dance' ain't wack. But it don' matter what you play cuz she can't hear it."

"She can't hear it? Should I turn it up?"

"Still won't do no good. She's deaf. She can't hear shit."

"She's deaf?" The realization hit me like a punch in the groin. "How do you know she's deaf?"

"I seen her talking to her man using sign language and shit." Heaven moved her fingers in the air pretending that she was signing a message to me. "I was telling you to eat a dick in sign language."

"Nice. Thanks for that." All of a sudden, I felt truly remorseful for playing all those songs for her. Though it made perfect sense, I had no idea that she was deaf. "Well, I've worked with her five or six times, and she still hasn't tipped me or any other DJ at the club."

"She hasn't tipped you?" Heaven asked with more than a hint of incredulity. "She don' make no money. The bitch is deaf. She can't hustle cuz the customers don't know sign language. Damn."

"I suppose you're right. Now I feel like a dick."

"You should." She shook her head and sauntered back to the dressing room, moving her index finger back and forth in a "tick-tick" motion while mouthing the chorus of the song.

When the shift ended, I didn't bother waiting at the door to be tipped out by Barbie. I felt that I should apologize for mocking her, but since I didn't know sign language, it wouldn't have made much of a difference. I attempted to rationalize my behavior by acknowledging the fact that she didn't actually hear the music that I was playing for her, but that didn't lighten my conscience. On her way out, she walked by the booth, but I avoided her and pretended to be busy packing up my CD cases. I never saw her again after that shift. I'd like to think that she found a job at a strip club for the disabled where she'd have an equal opportunity to make as much money as the other dancers, but, sadly, a club like that doesn't exist.

Dick Has a Sore Throat

It was inevitable. Bound to happen sooner or later. I had had sexual intercourse with twenty different strippers in six months. Venereal disease was the unavoidable outcome. I'm not trying to boast here. I've never been considered a stud and never will be. I'm not even a handsome man. Women usually tell me I'm "unconventionally handsome," which is a polite way of saying you're not very attractive. But, unless you're physically deformed, it's very easy to get laid when you work at a strip club. In fact that's the only time one ever gets laid at a strip club unless you're a drug dealer or you're paying for it. Honestly, it was easier to score at a strip club than it was in college, and I'd wager that the girls at the club were less intoxicated. My tried and true line was simply, "So, what are you doing after work? You want to come over and smoke a joint?" It worked every time. Sometimes we wouldn't even take the time to smoke the joint. I can only wish it was that easy for me now. But it's not like I didn't use protection when I had sex. I'm not an idiot. I wore condoms with most of my sex partners, but as the Center for Disease Control pamphlets proclaim: The only way to be 100 percent sure of eliminating your risk of contracting STDs is to abstain from sex. Abstinence. That's realistic. Sure. I'll abstain from sex, and while I'm at it, perhaps I'll become a Mormon and wear magic underwear too. I recognized the fact that I was commingling with loose women, but I thought that I had safeguarded myself to the best of my drunken ability with the frequent use of prophylactics. Sadly, I was mistaken.

It was a day before my twenty-ninth birthday when I realized that something was burning downstairs during a routine urination. As usual, I had drunk a bit too much the night before and was rudely awoken by the urgent pressure of a full bladder. Stumbling to the toilet, my eyes hardly adjusting to the daylight, I stood there at ten in the morning with my penis in my hand. A strong yellowish-orange stream of urine shot into the toilet, and I suddenly came to the startling realization that something was tingling down there. This pee did not feel like a normal pee. There was something "tingly" about this pee. Now I didn't immediately jump to conclusions and assume that I had contracted some hideous venereal disease, though the idea was floating around in the back of my mind. Rather I felt that I was having one of those hot morning pees. It made sense that my bladder had been full of warm urine all night and now it tingled the thin walls of my urethra upon exit. It's a completely natural occurrence, especially after a night of heavy drinking. Yet, I still felt that something was awry, and as I returned to bed, I attempted to mollify my worried mind by rationalizing that if indeed I had a venereal disease, I wouldn't merely experience a tingling sensation, I'd be forced to my knees by the excruciating pain of my scorching junk. And since that didn't occur, I reasoned that there was nothing seriously amiss. It wasn't till about three hours later, when I officially awoke and right before my second urination of the day, that I discovered a whitish fluid leaking out of the head of my penis. There was no doubt about it. This was a discharge. There was fucking pus leaking out of the head of my penis. I freaked out and ran to the kitchen, grabbed a half-full bottle of vodka, and emptied its contents into my dickhole. That gave me the scorching sensation that had vexed me before, and the vodka burned so severely that I had to shove my dick under the faucet of the kitchen sink and pour cold water over it for the next five minutes. I was glad I was alone as this would be a difficult scenario to explain to a woman whom you had just had sex with the night before. I then took a shower and sat down in the tub vigorously scrubbing the head of my cock with a bar of soap. By the end of my hysterics, my dick was chafed and crimson red. But now, my suspicions were confirmed. I had definitely caught something. I didn't know what to do. I had never contracted a venereal disease before and had no idea how to deal with it. There was only one person that I could call for advice: my brother, Jeffrey. As a bartender at several leather bars in San Francisco's Castro neighborhood and a frequent visitor to highway rest stops throughout the country, he definitely had experience with these matters. I agitatedly dialed his number, praying that he would answer his phone.

"Hey, what's up, guy?" he said cheerfully.

"Hey, man, do you have a second? It's important," I responded with rising urgency in my voice.

"Yeah, sure. Are you okay?"

"Well, not exactly. I'm not dying or anything. Well, maybe. I don't know yet. But I think I caught something down there."

"Down there?"

"Yeah, I think I have syphilis or something along those lines."

"Syphilis?" he asked, laughing.

"Hey, this is a serious matter. It fucking burns when I piss, and I think I had a discharge."

"Hold on. How do you know you had a discharge?"

"How do I know? There is a milky fluid seeping out of the head of my cock. That's how I fucking know. Jesus. Do you want me to come over and show you?"

"Okay. Calm down. You're freaking out for no reason. If you're that worried, go to the clinic and get tested. You probably have gonorrhea."

"What? Gonorrhea? The clap? Holy shit. How the fuck did I get the clap? I thought only seventies porn stars got the clap."

"Well, that's what happens when you sleep with dirty birds."

"Oh my god. I can't believe this is happening." I felt myself begin to hyperventilate.

"Take it easy. Gonorrhea's not that big of a deal. I've had it four times. It just means your dick has a sore throat. They give you some antibiotics and it clears up in a week," he said with a nonchalance that I found infuriating.

"I can't fucking believe this is happening to me. I probably have AIDS."

"Guy, settle down. You don't have AIDS. Just go to the clinic tomorrow and get tested. You'll be fine."

He had to get back to work, so I hung up the phone and paced around my apartment, obsessively checking the head of my cock every two minutes to see if there was another discharge. Finally, I grabbed my laptop and googled the San Francisco City Clinic. Since it was Sunday, the clinic was closed. I had no other choice but to wait till the next morning to get my junk checked out. I didn't leave my apartment all day. I lay in bed with the blinds tightly shuttered and the lights off, a playlist consisting of alternating Smiths and Joy Division songs playing loudly on my stereo. All I could think of was Eddie Murphy describing herpes as something you keep forever, like luggage. I envisioned how my entire life would be dramatically altered when the doctor told me that I had herpes. How can someone possibly have a normal sex life with herpes? If you have any semblance of a scruple, aren't you supposed to inform your prospective sex partner of your condition prior to the sex act? I shuddered at the thought of ever having to be in that situation. I pictured myself firmly holding her hands in mine and staring directly into her eyes:

"Baby, there's something I must confess before we do this..."

I divulge my secret and, consequently, she runs around the room in hysterics, picking her clothes up off the floor and trying to vacate the premises as hastily as possible. Whenever sex requires a disclaimer, the outcome is rarely good. I tried not to think about it. I attempted to distract myself with three hours of Ren & Stimpy and some potent marijuana. It didn't help. In fact, it made things worse. The animated figures on the television resembled the insidious bacteria ravaging my precious genitals. I had to shut it off. Then I lay in bed, in silence, staring at the ceiling. It was four in the morning, January 22. I was twenty-nine years old. And my first birthday gift was a venereal disease. I began to weep bitter tears of shame.

Finally, I fell asleep and awoke several hours later around 9:30 AM. I threw on a shirt and jeans, ran out of my apartment, and caught the first cab I could find. The clinic was located in the South of Market neighborhood on 7th and Folsom and was only a ten-dollar cab ride away. In the back of the cab, I thought about how the City Clinic is a blessing for people without insurance. I asked the cab driver to drop me off on the corner so that he wouldn't discern my ultimate destination. But from my impatient twitching and sweat-covered brow, I'm sure he had a good idea. I walked briskly down 7th Street, and when I neared the clinic, I saw that there was a queue of about fifteen people waiting to get inside. Contemplating whether or not there might be a guest list and then chiding myself for thinking something so retarded, I took my position at the end of the line behind a portly, dark-skinned black man dressed in a red mink peacoat, red mink flat cap, and dark black sunglasses at 10:00 AM on a sunny San Francisco morning. When I walked up behind him, he slowly turned around, looked me over, and flashed a wide grin. His gold-capped teeth shone brightly in the sunlight.

"How you doin', bro?" he asked.

"Good. Thanks," I replied uneasily, forcing myself to smile.

"Well, you can't be doin' too good if you're standing in this line." With that he broke into a spasm of laughter, which quickly transformed into a fit of coughs and wheezes.

I nodded my head, hoping that by not answering him vocally he'd stop talking to me. I wished I had brought my headphones. Though I didn't feel like listening to music, I still could have put them on and not been bothered by anyone. He was still chatting away, and as I took account of him, I couldn't help but notice that he looked a lot like the comedian Bernie Mac. Well, a younger, obese, and "thugged-out" version of Bernie Mac in a red fur coat. The man must have weighed at least 350 pounds and was well over six and a half feet tall. But his most distinctive features were his tattoo of the words "West Side" in Old English letters across his throat, and his mouthful of gold teeth. Glancing down the line, I noticed that I wasn't the only anxious person waiting to get his junk checked out. Everyone seemed to be nervously checking the time on their watches or cellphones every five seconds, their left leg shaking uncontrollably, their right hand buried deep into their pockets playing with loose change, their head hung low with consternation. Their sentiment echoed my own, and I too was staring at the sidewalk, trying to avoid eye contact with anyone. Suddenly I felt a sharp shot of anxiety jolt my body as I realized that it was quite possible that someone I work with could be standing in this line or in the waiting room inside. I couldn't think of anything more humiliating than running into a random barback, ex-girlfriend, or, even worse, a dancer at the clinic. The rumors would spread like wildfire, and I would be a laughingstock for months. Maybe even years. I started to panic and was about to split and deal with my genital malady at a later date when my rational side took over. If a dancer were here, then that would mean that she caught something too and there's an "honor among thieves thing" that exists with people who work in the industry. I'm sure we'd give each other knowing glances from time to time, but this day would never be spoken of again, especially not in a public setting. I surveyed the queue, carefully looking for anyone I might know. Of the fifteen people, there were only two women in line, and I didn't recognize either one.

Gangsta Bernie Mac broke my rumination by stating, "Damn. My dick and balls be itchin' like crazy." He furiously scratched at his crotch, shaking his head. "Man, I took a piss this morning, looked at my dick, and the shit was red. For real. Red. Like a supersized twizzler. You ever seen a nigga with a red dick before?"

I wasn't sure if the question was rhetorical, but I offered up an answer regardless, "No, I can't say that I have."

211

"Hell no, you ain't seen a nigga with a red dick before. Cuz the shit ain't right. I tole my baby's momma, I gots to go and get my shit checked out. She starts trippin', throws a 40 at my head. I should have slapped the bitch, but I just left and came over here. Damn. What you got goin' on?"

"Umm, nothing really."

"Nothin'? You wouldn't be standing in this line if you ain't got nothin' goin' on." Even though this was practically the same joke that he had told moments before, it still produced the same laugh/cough/wheeze combo.

"No offense but I'd prefer not to discuss my medical concerns with you. You don't appear to be a doctor. I might be wrong but most doctors don't wear red fur coats."

He looked at me angrily for a second and then broke into a wide, gold-toothed grin and replied, "You know what I hate about comin' here? We're across the street from a motherfuckin' elementary school."

I didn't notice that until he pointed it out, but sure enough, across the street from the City Clinic was Bessie Carmichael Elementary School. We watched a group of about ten kids playing a game with a large red ball in the playground. When someone kicked the ball over to the fence, a kid ran over to fetch it and paused to stare at the people standing in the long queue across the street. I watched his teacher walk over, grasp his little hand in hers, and guide him back over to the group. I imagined her admonishing him:

"Listen, Benjamin. I have something very important to tell you. You need to keep your grades up, never do drugs, and never have sex. If you do drugs and have sex then you'll end up over there like those sad, diseased people." She grasped his neck firmly with her left hand and forced him to stare at the luckless lot standing across the street, and with her right hand she pointed menacingly at us.

I slipped on my sunglasses and glanced at my cellphone in a feeble attempt to avoid the accusing eyes of the passersby. They looked at us as if we had leprosy. This was becoming unbearable. I felt like a prisoner at a Nazi concentration camp being marched into the showers. My mind was racing, and I started to experience psychosomatic feelings of the venereal disease slowly poisoning my other vital organs. I chainsmoked one cigarette after another, but it did little to calm my nerves. I could have shot a gram of dilaudid and listened to an entire Massive Attack record, and I still would have been on edge.

After about an hour of waiting, we finally entered the doors of the clinic. A large nurse, sitting at a desk near the front door, told us to take a number, much like you do at a delicatessen, and wait for it to be called. The back wall of the waiting room was covered, floor-to-ceiling, with pamphlets about safe sex and venereal disease. I chose to bypass the reading material and quietly slipped into a chair in the back corner. The waiting room was filled with people and there were only a few open chairs left. The crowd was rather diverse. From white businessmen wearing designer suits to Mexican gangbangers and tranvestite prostitutes, there were people here from all segments of society. It amused me to think that venereal disease is the force that unites us all. The radio was tuned to KMEL, a soul music station, and the Kool & the Gang song "Get Down On It" was playing through tiny speakers in the ceiling. Though it's a bit played out, I normally didn't mind hearing that song. But this morning, I found it extremely irritating. I kept thinking that's the reason I was here in the first place: getting down on it too many times without protection. Now I really wished I had brought my headphones. The wall on the right was curiously adorned with a large mural of a tropical jungle featuring various jungle animals, like a toucan, a jaguar, and a baboon. I didn't really see how the mural fit, but I liked the fact that it added some color to this dull, antiseptic environment. I envisioned the jaguar jumping out of the painting and savaging the people ahead of me in line. That would speed things up.

It was now almost 11:30, and I had been waiting over an hour. I heard one of the middle-aged nurses announce in an apathetic tone the number "88." I looked down at the crumpled piece of paper in my hand and sighed heavily when I discovered that it had the number "118" printed on it. Without my headphones or any non-STD reading material, I just sat there vacantly staring ahead, trying my hardest to pretend I was somewhere else. I focused my attention on the TV mounted on the wall above the nurses' desks. There was no sound, but the program was close-captioned so I was able to follow it. I watched for about ten minutes before I realized what was actually going on. The clinic had produced their own dramatic films of different situations when a protagonist would contract a venereal disease and then be forced to confess their misdeeds to their spouse or partner. In this particular episode, a married black man had been carrying on a secret love affair with another man and contracted AIDS. Now he had to reveal to his wife that he was having a homosexual affair and ask her to get tested for her own safety. It was surely going to destroy their marriage, but he could not keep secrets like this from his wife anymore. The video took pains to illustrate the moral turpitude of living one's life on the "down-low." I was unfamiliar with that term but saw how the lesson of the video was applicable to the lives of many people in the room. Without warning, a monotone voice announced, "118." It took me a moment before I realized that my number had been called, but as soon as I did, I jumped to my feet and rapidly walked to the front of the room, my hand holding my ticket high up in the air as if I had won a raffle. The VD raffle. Congratulations, number 118, you have syphilis.

"Hi, I'm number 118," I said excitedly, handing the ticket to a large black female nurse.

"Okay. Follow me," she said, frowning.

I followed her down a corridor to a small examination room.

She opened the door and pointed to two blue plastic chairs. "Sit down and wait. The doctor will be here in a few minutes."

I sat down on the chair directly underneath the anatomical poster of a man's penis and inspected the room. It looked like a regular doctor's office. I didn't see any bloodstains on the floor or aborted fetuses in the trashcan. In fact, it was much more sterile than I thought a city clinic would be. I spied a metal container filled with condoms and lube on the counter across from me and quickly grabbed a handful as the doctor walked into the room. She was a very attractive Asian in her early thirties. Wonderful. I get to show my diseased penis to an attractive woman. I might as well get used to it.

"Hi, my name is Dr. Green. And you are?"

"Uh. Hi. Um. My name's Dave."

"Hi, Dave. What brings you here today?"

I was at a loss for words. It's not often that you find yourself spending your birthday at the City Clinic with pus leaking out of the head of your cock while chatting with a beautiful Asian woman. It took me a few moments to respond. "Umm. I experienced a slight burning sensation when I urinated this morning and am worried that I might have caught something."

"Okay. I have a few questions that I need you to answer." She asked me a series of questions about my sexual preference, the number of sexual partners I've had in the past year, whether I had hired a sex worker, and if I had ever had a venereal disease before. She seemed slightly unnerved when I told her how many sexual partners I had in the past year, but she did not comment. Once the interrogation was over, she put her folder on the counter, slipped on a pair of latex gloves, and said, "All right. Let's pull down your pants and have a look."

I wasn't expecting her to be so blunt. I suppose I didn't know how it would go down, but I didn't think it'd be like this. I expected her to leave the room and allow me to disrobe and slip into a gown and then she would be able to examine me. "So, you want me to just pull my pants down right here?"

"Yes, that would work."

"It would work," I laughed nervously. The reason I was nervous was that I felt my dick begin to stiffen as soon as she said, "pull down your pants." To my chagrin, there was something about an attractive woman wearing a doctor's white coat that I found extremely arousing at that moment. I wasn't too surprised because I usually have at least three awkward boners a day. Considering the circumstance, I didn't think I'd get one at the clinic.

"Umm, can I go to the bathroom? I have to pee." I didn't really have to go, but I was trying to buy myself some time.

"Well, actually that's not a good idea because the urine would wash out any type of discharge that may be there. I'd rather examine you before you do that."

"Oh, okay." Reluctantly, I stepped forward, unbuttoned my pants, and pulled out my semi-hard penis. The doctor didn't seem to pay any attention to my tumescence and instead was focusing her attention on the head of my penis.

"Yep. Looks like we have a discharge," she announced triumphantly, holding up her index finger to show me a pus-like substance.

As soon as I saw the discharge on the tip of her finger, my arousal vanished and my dick shrank to a third of its usual size. "Holy shit. That's disgusting."

"Well, you definitely have something. That's for sure. We just don't know what yet. I'm going to examine this under the microscope to see if I can tell whether it's gonorrhea or chlamydia. In the meantime, please take this cup to the bathroom and bring back a urine sample." She put a plastic cup into a brown paper bag and handed it to me.

"Okay. Thanks. Is there a bathroom back here?"

"There's a bathroom in the waiting room. When you have your sample, bring it to the nurse at the front desk and she'll escort you back to this room."

I left the examination room and walked out to the waiting area with my brown paper bag and urine cup. I couldn't believe my life had come to this. And the worst part was that I didn't even have to go to the bathroom. I figured I might as well try. Perhaps being in front of a toilet would cause me to want to go. As I walked around the rows of chairs, I noticed that there were quite a few people with brown paper bags in their hands. I guess I wasn't alone. The bathroom was on the smaller side and consisted of one stall and one urinal. The stall was occupied with a man who sounded like he was in the throes of terrible intestinal distress. He was loudly moaning, and every few seconds I heard a wet fart noise and the sound of liquid shit splattering against the porcelain bowl. The sound was not only disgusting but the stench was unbearable. I didn't even try to pee. I returned to the waiting room and sat down in the first open chair I could find.

"Hey, Sanchez, you waiting to pee? Me too," said a familiar feminine voice.

I looked up and did a double take when I saw Chyna sitting to my right holding a brown paper bag in her hand. She and I currently worked together at Teasers, but in the past I had worked with her at several other clubs, including the Doll House and Foxys. Chyna had a petite figure and wore her hair in a blonde weave with one side in tight braids that softly contrasted with her mocha complexion. I had never seen her without a full face of makeup, and this occasion was no exception. In fact, it seemed like she had purposely dressed up to come to the City Clinic just in case she might meet a suitor.

"Oh, hey you. What are you doing here?" I asked, trying my best to minimize the awkwardness.

"The same reason you're here. My pussy itches from some dirty dick," she said with an insidious laugh. "You by yourself?"

"Uhh, yeah. You?"

"I smoked a blunt, dropped my kids off at my baby's daddy, and came over here. Been here since 8:30."

Chyna couldn't have been much older than twenty-two. I shuddered to think of the type of role model she was as a parent. "Well, you look great for having woken up so early."

"Sanchez, you know I always look fine. I don't care where I'm going. So who you been hookin' up with? I seen you talking to Desire. And I thought, hell no, he don't want none of that. That ho is nasty. You know when she worked at Foxys she sucked Pepper's dick?"

218

"Haha. I didn't hook up with Desire. I talk to lots of girls at work about music and other work-related matters."

"Don't lie to me, boy. You a player. I hear people talkin'. Girls talk in the dressin' room. I ain't finna tell you what they be sayin', but they talk. A lot."

"Well, I wouldn't believe everything you hear. Things can be taken out of context and that's how vicious rumors are started. Case in point, the other day I was chatting with—"

"Hold up. I gotta piss." She hastily stood up and gracefully walked in her six-inch heels towards the woman's lavatory. After a few minutes, she returned holding her brown paper bag up in the air like a trophy. "I was waiting twenty minutes to piss. Damn. Now I can get the fuck out of here. Peace out, Sanchez."

Before she turned to leave, I said, "Chyna, let's forget we saw each other here this morning, okay?"

She cracked a wry smile. "Okay. You know what helps me to forget? Weed. You got any smoke?"

"No, why would I bring weed to the clinic?"

"I dunno. So you can smoke it. How much money you got?"

"Wait a second. Are you trying to extort me?"

"Do you want me to forget I seen you or what?"

"Well, I saw you too. So if you tell people you saw me here, I'll say that I saw you here."

"Yeah, e'erbody knows I come here two or three times a month. I don't give a fuck if they know. How many times you been here, Sanchez? I don't think I e'er seen you up in here before."

She had me and she knew it. I reached for my wallet and pulled out two $20 bills. "Okay, I only have $40, but I'll give it to you if you forget that we saw each other today and we'll never talk about this experience again. Deal?"

She snatched the money from my hand and smiled that wry smile again. I found it difficult to trust that smile. "Sanchez, you got yourself a deal. I didn't see nobody up in the clinic today." She turned around and walked behind the back row of chairs on her way to deliver the nurse her urine-filled cup.

I didn't trust Chyna at all, but there was little I could do except bribe her. Hopefully, the money would buy her discretion, but I was skeptical. I waited for another ten minutes or so before I had to pee. Luckily, the stall was vacant and the odor had dissipated somewhat. I filled the cup with warm urine, carefully placed it back into the bag, and quickly left the bathroom to give it to the nurse. She told me to follow her back to the exam room where I found Dr. Green writing notes on her clipboard. "Hi, Doctor, I have a cup of pee for you. You know, I never thought I'd say that."

Perhaps she didn't find my joke humorous or wasn't paying attention, but with a serious expression, she replied, "So, after examining the slide under the microscope, I could tell that you have gonorrhea. I want you to get a blood sample as well, so we can test for other sexually transmitted infections."

I was devastated by the news. I knew I had caught something, but I didn't realize I had caught many things. What am I? A grab bag full of diseases? A VD swap meet? Alarmed, I asked the doctor, "What do you mean other infections? How many can a person have?"

The doctor sensed my agitation and responded using a much softer tone. "I didn't mean to frighten you. It's possible that you could have contracted two different infections, so it's a good idea to do a blood test just to make sure we have our bases covered. But before you leave, we'll give you antibiotics to treat the gonorrheal infection."

Her words did nothing to alleviate my concerns. I had already convinced myself that I had AIDS and was trying to determine whom I was going to will my record collection to. Dr. Green led me to a small lab where I had two tubes of blood drawn. I didn't even wince when the nurse inserted the needle. At this point, the pain was meaningless. They could drain me of my diseased life-blood, and it would only serve to hasten the dying process. The nurse had me fill out a form and choose a password, and instructed me to call in two weeks to get the results of the tests. She said that they would contact me if the AIDS test turned out positive. I was thrilled to wait two weeks to learn my fate. To treat the gonorrhea, she gave me an antibiotic called Suprax and told me to abstain from sexual activity for the next week. That wasn't going to be difficult. I was so disgusted with myself that I couldn't fathom masturbation, let alone sexual intercourse. Finally, she said that it'd be a good idea to inform any sexual partner that I have had in the past month that I have a gonorrheal infection, so they can get tested as well. That was not going to be a simple task. Not only was my reputation at stake, but also my livelihood was at risk. A couple of the girls I hooked up with in the past month were married to ex-convicts. To my chagrin, I found out about this after the fact. I decided it was best to keep my little secret to myself.

The next day, I had to work the Tuesday night shift at Teasers. I brought a Suprax in my pocket just so I could be sure to take my evening dose at the right time. I was following the doctor's orders verbatim.

While it still burned slightly when I urinated, I had stopped looking for evidence of a discharge because now I found the whole situation extremely depressing. I arrived at the club a bit earlier than usual and decided to use the rear entrance as to avoid having to talk to anyone. As I walked to the back door, I smelled the unmistakable aroma of potent marijuana. I looked around for the source and found Chyna sitting in a black Honda Civic sucking on a blunt. The driver's side window was cracked open and thick plumes of grayish smoke escaped through the narrow opening. I hurried my step and tried to walk by unnoticed, but unfortunately she had already spotted me. Rolling down the window, she leaned out of the car and yelled:

"What up, Sanchez? Does it still hurt when you pee?" She laughed so hard when she said this that she almost tumbled out of the window.

I pretended not to hear her and waved as I walked by her car. Though I couldn't make a positive identification, it looked like Gangsta Bernie Mac was sitting in the passenger seat.

"Sanchez, I'm jus' messin' wit u. You wanna smoke some of this blunt?"

"No, thanks. I have to get upstairs and set up for my shift. But you better be careful. I heard Randy's working tonight." Randy was the General Manager of Teasers. He was a diminutive man, standing barely over 5'4", with a fearsome cocaine habit and an even more fearsome Napoleon complex. He had a reddish-brown mullet with feathered layers on the sides that he had worn proudly since the eighties, and rumor had it that he had used so much tanning spray over the years that his skin was permanently dyed an orange hue. Even without the cocaine, he had a mercurial disposition. Randy suffered no fools and would unleash his fury on any of his employees without the slightest provocation. You never knew what would set him off, which is the reason most people hid from him when he made his rounds. If a door guy saw Randy walking in his snakeskin cowboy boots towards the club, he'd warn the managers over the radio and they'd hide out in the bathroom waiting for him to leave. There really was no place for the DJ to hide. He just had to pray for mercy, which Randy rarely dispensed. I heard that he once fired a popular DJ for playing Lou Reed's "Satellite of Love." We found out later that Randy had caught his ex-wife blowing a bouncer in his Corvette and that song was playing on the car stereo at the time. Simply put, Randy was someone you did your best to avoid at all costs. One surefire way to piss him off and be instantly terminated was to smoke marijuana during your shift. Randy despised marijuana with a passion. If he smelled even the faintest odor of it, he'd accost any employee in the vicinity and shine his penlight in their eyes to see if he could tell whether their eyes were red. He called this procedure "Randy's Roadblock," and everyone lived in fear of it. Chyna seemed undaunted by my warning.

"Randy can eat a fat dick. I ain't scared of that motherfucker."

With that, she took an egregious puff on her blunt, stuck her head back inside the car, and rolled up the window. I continued on my way and entered the club through the back door. Without encountering anyone, I ran upstairs to the DJ booth and came upon Derek, the day shift DJ, packing up his CD case. I liked Derek because he was too inexperienced and, quite honestly, too simple to ever be considered a threat. As a night shift DJ, you need to be constantly aware of the position of the DJs beneath you. All strip club DJs are a scheming lot who would stab each other in the back without hesitation if it meant earning more money on better shifts. But simple Derek had no aspirations to work the night shifts. He'd often remark, "Night shifts are too busy and too dangerous for me."

"Yo, Sanchez, what's up, man?" he asked, sounding genuinely excited to see me.

"Not too much. How was the day shift?"

"It was good. A little slow in the beginning but picked up the last two hours. You have a nice crowd up in here now."

I scanned the room and saw that most of the tables near the front row were filled with perverts. "Yeah, it looks like a good crowd. Thanks for getting them warmed up." I began to remove one of my CD cases from my backpack when I noticed Derek anxiously staring at me and fidgeting with his lighter. "Hey, dude, is everything okay?"

He shuffled towards me, staring at the ground, mumbling, "Umm. Can I show you something?"

"Yeah, sure. What is it?"

"Well, umm, I gots this problem. You know, a problem down…there. And was wondering if you'd take a look at it."

"A problem down there? What are you talking about, Derek?"

"Well, I heard you was at the clinic yesterday, and you know about this type of shit, and I don't know, I thought that…I thought that…maybe I could show you my dick and you can tell me if I got summin'."

I couldn't believe what I was hearing. That lying bitch. That soulless harlot. I knew she couldn't be trusted. "Derek, tell me, did Chyna happen to mention that she saw me at the clinic yesterday?"

"Nah."

"Okay, then. Who told you that I was at the clinic yesterday?"

"Umm, Star told me."

"Star? And how'd she know?"

"She said she heard from Mercedes that your nuts had swelled up and you had to go to the clinic and have 'em drained."

"My nuts were swollen, huh?"

"Yeah, she said they was like the size of a mini basketball. Damn, did that shit hurt?"

"Derek, my testicles weren't swollen. That's not the reason I was there. Regardless, how did Mercedes hear about this?"

"I dunno. I heard it from Star, but she said all the girls be talking about it today."

"That's good to hear." I was so angry that I felt like beating his simple face into a bloody mass of torn tissue and broken teeth. But this wasn't his fault. Gossip moves through a strip club like cocaine at a Kiss concert. I'm sure Chyna had told one or two girls about seeing me at the clinic and within an hour everyone at the club knew about it.

"So, can I show you my dick? I got this red bump on it and I don't know what it is."

"No, you can't show me your dick. I'm not a doctor. You should go to the clinic and show them your dick. Jesus."

"Come on, man. I been freaking out all day. If my girl sees this shit, I'm done. I can't lose her. Come on, please."

"Derek, you need to take this girl off the stage and put up the next one." He was so concerned with having me look at his dick that he had forgotten that he was still working. In a panic, he quickly jumped over to the mixer, faded out the 50 Cent song that was playing, announced the next girl to the stage, and started playing some rap song that I didn't recognize. He then turned around and resumed pleading with me.

"Sanchez, please, I'm beggin' you, man. Just take one look. I don't have anyone else I can talk to about this."

225

I sympathized with his plight. I was in a similar situation a couple days ago, but at least I had my brother to confide in. Poor Derek had no one but me. Begrudgingly, I consented. "Okay, I'll take a quick look, but as I said before, I'm not a doctor. I don't even know what to look for."

He was instantly relieved and began to unbutton his pants. "Thanks so much, man. I totally owe you one." He pulled out his penis and rolled it around in his hand, trying to find the mysterious red bump. "It's too dark in here. I can't find it. Do you have a lighter?"

"Ugh, okay," I said, unable to conceal my disgust. I lit my lighter and held it above his penis.

"Okay, that's it. Right there. See that bump? What is it?"

I looked closer at the tiny red bump on the base of his penis, but I was unable to diagnose what it was. "Derek, I think that's a pimple. I'm not sure, but that's what I think it is."

"A zit?" he said incredulously.

"Yeah, a zit."

"Nah, man. It hurts too bad to be a zit. I think it's herpes. Look at it."

I leaned over and took one more look at the sore on his penis and said, "Dude, I'm not a doctor. I think it's a zit, but you should…"

"What the fuck is going on over here?" boomed a loud voice behind us.

Startled, we both turned around and found Randy standing in the doorway of the booth with a look of complete and utter revulsion on his orange face.

"What the fuck is this faggot shit?" he screamed, aggressively wiping his nose with his right hand. He was so angry that spit was forming in the corners of his mouth, making him look like a rabid Oompa Loompa.

Like everyone else, I was scared to death of Randy. And once provoked, it was practically impossible to reason with him. I knew Derek was going to be of little help, so I had to think of something fast.

"Randy, this is totally not what you think. I know it looks bad, but it's not what you think. Derek, over here, burned himself on the mixer. You know, it's been heating up a lot lately due to overuse or maybe faulty wiring. I'm not sure which, but I suffered a mild burn the last time I worked. A lot of DJs have been complaining about it. It's a ticking time bomb."

By this time, Derek had pulled his pants up and was staring at Randy, paralyzed with fear. Randy stood there fuming, but I could tell that he was listening to me. My excuse wasn't a total fabrication. The last time I had worked, one of the day shift DJs mentioned that the mixer was unusually hot during his shift. I noticed that it was a bit warm, but I didn't feel it was necessary to bring it up with management. Until now.

"I was worried that Derek might have sustained an injury from the club's mixing board, and in order to avoid any type of lawsuit situation, I told him that I would take a look to see how serious the burn is. It's not that bad. I think Derek may have been overreacting a bit. Right, Derek?"

With his body still frozen and unable to speak, Derek managed to move his head up and down. I wasn't sure whether Randy was buying my explanation. He was a difficult person to read. He just stood there eyeing the two of us suspiciously.

I continued, "I don't want the club to have to suffer through a prolonged and expensive lawsuit, so I was just trying to help out. As a witness, I was trying to pre-empt any kind of legal situation here."

Still looking at us warily, Randy ambled over to the mixing board. He reached out, gingerly touched it, and instinctively wrenched his hand back. "Damn, you're right, this fucking thing is hot. We're gonna have to replace it before someone gets hurt."

"That's a really good idea," I said, shaking my head. I looked over at Derek and noticed that he was still moving his head up and down from before.

"So, you two weren't trying to suck eachother's dicks. I won't stand for any faggot bullshit in my clubs."

"No, sir. I assure you that there was no faggot bullshit going on in here."

"Okay, then. Thanks for telling me about the mixer. I'll have it replaced tomorrow. Will you be all right with it tonight?"

"Yes, I think I can manage. But thanks for replacing it."

He flashed us one more wary glance and turned to leave when I stopped him, "Randy, hold on a second. When I was walking over here I smelled some marijuana smoke coming from one of the cars parked near the back door. I think it was coming from a black Honda Civic. I don't know who is smoking drugs outside, but I just don't want the club to get in trouble."

Randy's eyes lit up when he heard the word "marijuana." "What time did you smell the marijuana?"

"It was about fifteen minutes ago. Maybe less."

Randy nodded his head and slapped my shoulder with his right hand. "You're one of the good ones. I'll remember this." He bounded out of the DJ booth on his way to enforce his martial law. I smiled as I watched him leave. I honestly hoped that he didn't fire Chyna. After all, she was a single mother. Rather, I hoped that she would be banished from working on Broadway and forced to work at the deplorable clubs in the Tenderloin for a year.

Though my gonorrhea cleared up in a week, it took about a month of damage control to dispel the rumors circulating through the club. Derek was so appreciative that I had saved his job that he appointed himself my PR person and made it his mission to clear my reputation. In a few weeks, the girls had completely forgotten about my venereal misfortune and were spreading rumors about something else. It's rare that news lasts long in a strip club, thanks to narcotics and attention deficit disorder. I never found out what happened to Chyna, but on my next three visits to the San Francisco City Clinic, I made sure to keep an eye out for her.

Kashmir

"Fuck. I'm late," I muttered under my breath as I rushed to the train station at Church and Market. One of my myriad shortcomings is that I tend to talk to myself out loud when I'm anxious. This habit of mine used to make me feel self-conscious because I thought I looked like an insane person walking down the streets yelling audibly at myself with my hands wildly gesticulating in the air. However, after living in San Francisco and encountering someone at least once a day screaming out loud with their pants around their ankles and defecating on the sidewalk, I realized that most people paid little attention to my harmless ramblings. My Saturday night shift at the Ruby Club started at 7:00 PM, and it was just after 6:30 PM, which should have given me more than enough time, but I really wanted to get a burrito before I went to work. I hadn't eaten anything at all that day and there was no way I'd be able to deal with fifty strippers without some nourishment. Drugs can sustain one's appetite only so much. El Castillito, my favorite tacqueria, was located on Church Street, a couple blocks from the train station. If I ran and there was no queue, I'd be able to buy a burrito and make it back to the station just in time for the 6:45 downtown train. I booked it down Church Street, and when I got to El Castillito, I was relieved to find only two people standing in line in front of me. When it was my turn to order, I requested my usual.

"Hi, can I have a vegetarian burrito with black beans and no sour cream please?" San Francisco tacquerias aren't renowned for their hygiene standards, and I've learned from dire past experiences to steer clear of the sour cream.

"No crema?" the youthful Mexican cook asked, obviously not hearing me the first time.

"Si, no crema por favor." I repeated in Spanish so he'd be sure to remember. I walked over to the cashier, paid in advance, and watched him shove a handful of tortilla chips into a plastic bag and gingerly place the foil-wrapped burrito on top. The cashier handed me the bag along with my change, and I set off in a mad dash to the train station. I practically slid down the staircase and barely slipped through the doors of the M train as they were about to close. Breathing a sigh of relief, I sank back into the hard plastic seat and shoved a couple chips in my mouth. My manager was not very empathetic when it came to tardiness, and this definitely wasn't the first time I was running late.

I ended up making it to the front door of the club five minutes before my shift started, and Tony, one of the bouncers, held the door open for me as I ran upstairs to the booth. I hastily unpacked my CD books and threw on a trance compilation while I waited for the house mom to come upstairs and write the dancer list on the whiteboard. The house moms served as the liaisons for the dancers and management, and it was prudent to stay on their good side because you never knew when you might need them to help you out. Autumn was working as house mom that night. She and I had worked together for years—long before she became management—and we had a close relationship. Most house moms were former dancers who either gained too much weight or were simply too old to continue dancing. Autumn was in the latter category, but she was well aware that it was time for her to retire and become a house mom. I was in the process of unwrapping my burrito when she entered the booth.

"Hey, sexy, how you doin' tonight?" I asked.

"I'm fine."

"I know you're fine, but how you doin'?"

She laughed. "I'm doing good. What you got? A burrito?"

"Yeah, I went to Castillito. You wanna bite?"

"Yeah, I'd love one." She took the burrito from me and was about to take a bite but then suddenly stopped. "Gross, you ordered sour cream."

"No. I didn't. I explicitly asked in Spanish for no sour cream. What the fuck?" She handed me the burrito and to my chagrin, I discovered that it was filled with sour cream. "Fuck. I hate sour cream."

"I know. Me too," she said while writing the dancers' names on the whiteboard in flawless cursive.

"Wow, there are a lot of girls working tonight."

"Yeah, I counted about forty before I came up here. There'll probably be at least twenty more in a couple hours."

I was starving and knew that this was going to be a long shift. I had no other choice but to eat the sour-cream-infested burrito.

"How is it?"

"You know, it's not that bad," I replied while shoving the last couple bites into my mouth. "I don't usually like sour cream, but this time it's all right."

"I'll take your word for it because I love Castillito. So, the first dancer tonight will be Destiny, okay?"

"Yeah. That's cool." I remembered that Destiny liked to dance to Incubus and flipped through my book of rock CDs looking for their new album. Autumn smacked my ass as she left the booth, and I announced that Destiny would be the first dancer onstage. About two hours into the shift, I felt a deep, unnatural rumbling in the pit of my stomach followed by a dull painful feeling. Though I was slightly unnerved, I ignored it, flipped on the dancer's next song, and then felt another unmistakably sharp pain in my gut. My stomach was not feeling good at all. I knew I shouldn't have eaten that burrito. I contemplated switching to a longer song and going to the bathroom, but then Alfredo—one of the club's bouncers—walked into the booth. Alfredo was, without exaggeration, a hulk of a man. He stood about 6'6" and weighed at least 280 pounds. His face was a battlefield of hypertrophic scars, and with his short dark hair, he reminded me of the actor who played Luca Brasi in the movie *The Godfather*. I'm not quite sure if he was actually Italian, but he did give a convincing portrayal.

"Hey, man, do you have any smoke? I'm out tonight," he asked, sounding like a New York City mobster from the 1970s.

"Yeah, yeah. Give me a minute."

Alfredo was always out of marijuana. I had worked with the guy for over two years and supported his drug habit the entire time. He never had any marijuana. Never. He worked at a strip club in San Francisco. A blind man could find drugs in less than five minutes at this place, but for some reason, Alfredo never seemed to have any luck. I fumbled in my backpack, found my Sneak-A-Toke, and tossed it to him. It looked like a tiny black bullet in his massive palm.

"Thanks, buddy. I'll bring it back in a minute," he mumbled, and lumbered out of the booth.

By this time, my stomach was in knots. I felt a steady series of sharp stabbing pains, as if someone kept punching me repeatedly in the same spot. I knew I was going to have to use the bathroom at some point, but I was doing my best to delay it. Although it was a plus that the upstairs bathroom had a single toilet, it was also gender neutral, and at this time of night, it was most likely disheveled and filthy, and undoubtedly there was a queue. I stuck my head out the door of the booth and, sure enough, there were four people in line for the restroom. Fuck. This was going to be a rough night. My stomach continued to rumble and I could tell that diarrhea was imminent. The situation was becoming drastic. I was on the verge of explosion and had to get to a bathroom in the next few minutes. I'd play a long song for the next dancer and use my position as DJ to cut in front of the people waiting in line for the bathroom. Slightly relieved that I had a plan, I took a deep breath, pulled myself together, and looked to see who was appearing onstage next. Gigi was coming up next. I loved Gigi. She and I had hooked up several times in the past but never actually dated. She always said "familiarity breeds contempt," which is the reason she avoided monogamous relationships. I didn't mind. Though she was my type exactly—dark hair, pale skin, buxom—I didn't want to date someone I worked with. Employee relationships are usually frowned upon at most strip clubs but it's rarely a good idea for any workplace. I knew Gigi liked to dance to trip-hop and was flipping through my book looking for Tricky's *Maxinquaye* CD when she sauntered into the booth.

"Hey, sexy, what are you going to play for me?" She grabbed me by the waist and started slowly kissing the back of my neck.

"Hey, Gigi. How you doin'?" I turned around and embraced her. Even with my bowels in their current state, I still found her incredibly attractive.

"I'm doin' okay. You're looking sexy tonight. Are those new jeans?"

"No, I don't think so. Maybe." It was difficult to pay attention with my stomach in such pain. I tried to play it off and did my best to act composed. "What do you feel like dancing to?"

"I dunno. What do you think would make me look sexy up there?"

"I don't think you need much help with that. You look sexy in your sleep."

"You're a fucking pervert. Didn't you fuck me when I was passed out at your house?"

"I haven't the faintest clue what you're talking about." I had to clench my ass cheeks together because I felt the sudden jolt of hot liquid shit attempting to make a most ungraceful exit.

"Are you okay? You look paler than usual."

"Uh, I'm fuh-fine," I stuttered, still clenching my ass together struggling to hold back the brown tsunami forcing its way out. I took a deep breath and exhaled slowly. I couldn't imagine a worse scenario than shitting myself in front of one of the hottest dancers in the club. I would never live that down. I'd have to change my career.

"Do you have an extra smoke?" she asked as she walked over and put her hands on my waist.

I moved her hands away lest they distract me from my sphincter control, and reached for my backpack. I pulled out a pack of Parliaments and handed her a cigarette. "Here you are, my dear," I said, my ass clenched together so tightly that it sounded like I was holding my breath.

"Are you sure you're okay? You look sick or something."

"No, I'm totally cool," I replied, wiping a thin layer of sweat off my forehead and running my hand through my hair all in one motion. If I made one wrong move, my pants would be filled with diarrhea in a matter of seconds. I stood there, motionless, too petrified to move. *God, please finish that smoke and leave* was the only thought reverberating through my mind.

"Shit! Do I have to go onstage right now?"

"Yeah, yes, I think you do," I answered, holding my breath in, barely able to force the words out. I was seconds away from shitting my pants.

She mashed the cigarette out in the ashtray and asked, "So, what are you playing for me?"

"Um, uh, I'll play you some rock. Is that cool? I think we have a rock crowd out there tonight." I could barely hold it in at this point and was staring at her in desperation. All I could think was, *Just leave, you fucking moron. I don't care if you're beautiful. I'm about to shit myself in front of you. Just fucking leave.*

"Okay. Sounds good." She leaned over and planted a kiss on my lips. "Well, even though you're a freak sometimes, I still think you're sexy. Toodles." She winked at me and then exited the booth.

"Uh. Okay, s-see you later," I stammered, watching her ass rhythmically shake from side to side as she walked down the hallway. I hobbled over to my CD case with my ass cheeks held tightly shut, resembling a child with cerebral palsy first learning how to walk with his crutches and leg braces. In desperation, I grabbed the first CD I could find. Led Zeppelin. This would work. Zeppelin was most definitely rock and the majority of their songs were over four minutes in length. I threw it in the CD player and scrolled to the second song. "Kashmir." Perfect. This song was over eight minutes long, which would give me more than enough time to run to the bathroom and get back to the booth. I pressed play and grabbed the microphone:

"G-gentlemen, l-let's put those hands together for our next s-sexy dancer. Guh-give it up for Gigi."

I was barely able to spit out the words. I didn't stay to see whether she walked onstage. I made a bold dash for the bathroom at the end of the hall and luckily no one was waiting in line. I kicked open the door and, as expected, discovered that the bathroom was in a state of utter disrepair. The faucet was running, and the sink was filled with water, vomit, and paper towels. The floor was covered in urine and sodden toilet paper. And to make matters worse, some asshole had kicked the toilet seat off its hinges, leaving it hanging haphazardly over the left side of the commode. I tried to lock the door but gave up when I realized that another asshole had broken the lock. Wonderful. Not being able to hold back any longer, I yanked my pants down and hovered my ass precariously over the toilet bowl while using my right hand to hold the door shut. I enthusiastically released a jet stream of liquid shit and sighed with relief as my bowels evacuated. I cannot remember ever feeling so relieved to take a shit. Suddenly, the door handle moved and someone tried to enter, but I lurched forward and slammed the door shut with all my remaining strength.

"Hey, what the fuck?"

"There's someone in here," I bellowed, still holding the door shut tightly.

While a river of shit streamed steadily from my asshole, I listened to hear what part of the song we were at. I still had time. Robert Plant had just reached the chorus. I looked down between my legs and realized the front of the toilet bowl and the back of my pants were covered in shit. Flustered, I searched the room for a roll of toilet paper to clean up this awful mess, but as my luck would have it, the only roll had been ripped from its dispenser and lay on the ground soaked through with urine and water. I saw that someone had also torn open the paper towel holder, but at least they left a stack of towels on the corner of the sink. Once my bowels had emptied, I hopped forward, my pants down around my ankles dragging through the pool of urine on the floor, towards the sink. I grabbed a handful of paper towels and feverishly rubbed them up and down the crack of my ass, trying in vain to wipe off my shit-coated thighs. Even worse, my pants were shellacked in diarrhea and soaked from the urine on the floor and cleaning them was going to be a challenge. I wet another stack of paper towels in the sink and squirted hand soap over them before attempting to wipe the shit from my pants, but it was a lost cause. I had to locate a replacement pair of trousers. Standing there with my shitty pants around my ankles, still holding the door shut with my right hand, I remembered that Ryan, the daytime DJ, always kept a spare outfit in the booth. On more than one occasion, I ridiculed him for it, but now his spare trousers would be my salvation. Again someone tried to push open the door, but I leaned on it hard with my shoulder, slamming it shut.

"What the fuck, man? How long you gonna be in there?" shouted an angry voice.

"Take it easy. I'm almost done," I answered, sounding more than irritated. I took a few seconds to listen to the song to see how much time

I had left and formulate a plan of action. Robert Plant was singing something about his finding his Shangri-La. We were in the middle of the second verse, and I knew I had at least four minutes left. Filled with desperation, I surveyed my shit-soaked dystopia and shuddered at the thought of having to return here again. It was the middle of the song. I had to move fast. I snatched the remaining paper towels and formed a makeshift diaper so that my soiled crotch wouldn't come in contact with my skin. The night wasn't even over yet and this was already one of the most tragic experiences of my life. I yanked my pants up, buckled my belt tightly to hold in the paper towel diaper, and checked my ass in the mirror to see if there was a massive brown stain. Surprisingly, it wasn't that bad. I attempted to flush the toilet, but there was no way that was going to happen. In fact, I think it had been clogged before I had even come in here. Looking down on the unholy mess that I had created, I shook my head in disgust and reached into my pockets for some matches. At the very least, I could try to dissipate the ghastly odor. No dice. My matches were in the DJ booth. I attempted to wash my hands without touching the puke and water-filled basin and then opened the bathroom door to find a disgruntled yuppie in an Armani suit, his face contorted in a rictus of revulsion.

"Jesus Fucking Christ. It smells like a goddamn sewer in here," he said, pinching his nose.

The other two men in line swiftly performed an about-face and, I imagine, opted to use the downstairs bathroom. I didn't even bother to apologize. That mess in there was well beyond the realm of apology. I just walked as fast as I could to the DJ booth and shut and locked the door. Hastily, I rummaged through the cabinets along the back wall till I found Ryan's spare outfit which consisted of a nondescript pair of black trousers and a dark blue Polo shirt. He was quite a bit taller than me, but at this moment, my sartorial options were severely limited. I carefully removed my soiled pants and the paper towel diaper and buried them both deep inside the trash bin. Then, I slipped off my boxer briefs and tossed those in the trash as well. I grabbed some hand sanitizer off the counter, squirted it down my crack, and proceeded to clean my ass with Ryan's Polo shirt. After I felt sufficiently cleaned, I pulled on Ryan's pants and had to tuck at least five inches of fabric inside the leg so that no one would notice they were about three sizes too long. As "Kashmir" was nearing the grandiloquent crescendo of the final bridge, I leaned over the booth and watched Gigi crawl about the stage on all fours while men showered her with dollar bills. Since she had been onstage for nearly eight minutes, I didn't think it was necessary to play her a second song. I slowly faded out Plant's "oohs" and "yeahs" and asked the audience to give Gigi a closing round of applause before starting the next song. Over the next several hours, I made three more trips to the restroom. However, none of these subsequent visits were as violent or traumatic as the first one. When I returned to the booth after my third trip, I found Gigi and a blonde dancer named Sonya sitting on the couch, smoking my cigarettes. I could tell they were both very intoxicated by the way they were screeching every time they spilled their martinis on my CD books.

"Where have you been?" asked Gigi.

"I had to run to the bathroom."

"Number 1 or Number 2?" she asked, bursting into laughter.

"Number 3," I answered gravely.

"You're gross."

"What are you guys doing up here?"

"We want to give you a booty bump?"

"A what?"

"A booty bump."

"What's that?"

"You don't know?" They both burst into laughter this time. "I'll show you." Gigi pulled down Sonya's thong and positioned her over the couch so that her bare ass was up in the air. I shut and locked the door just in case one of my managers happened to be in the vicinity. Gigi produced a small bag of cocaine from her bra, licked her index finger, stuck it in the bag, and held it up so that I could see the small mound of blow on the tip of her finger. She then spread Sonya's ass cheeks apart and deftly inserted her finger into her asshole. Sonya squealed as Gigi jammed her finger inside of her. She pulled out her finger, licked it, and looked at me, smirking. "That's a booty bump. Now it's your turn."

"Umm, I don't think that's a good idea," I said, knowing full well that Gigi did not want to stick her finger anywhere near my asshole right now.

"Come on. Don't be a faggot. It's intense. You'll love it." She lurched towards me, dangling the small bag of cocaine up in the air.

I grabbed her and said, "No, I don't think so. I still have an hour left. I can't do blow right now."

"Come on, you're such a faggot. Do a booty bump."

"No, I can't."

"Fine, then I'll do one. Sonya, you want to give me a booty bump?" She pulled down her thong and lay over the couch with her ass spread open. I was so aroused that I had to adjust my pants. Someone should make "booty bump" porn, as I imagine it would be a top-selling genre. Sonya licked her finger, scooped up some blow, and shoved her finger

242

deep into Gigi's hole. Gigi squealed with delight and asked for another. I couldn't stop staring at the sight before me but reluctantly had to turn away to start the next song for the dancer onstage.

"You sure you don't want one?" Sonya asked, her finger still in Gigi's asshole.

"It's tempting but no. I'll take a regular bump though." Sonya sauntered over to the counter and dumped out the contents of the little bag. She used a free lap-dance card to cut up a couple lines and then rolled up an ATM receipt and handed it to me. I snorted a line and reared backwards from its strong bite. Gigi always had good coke.

"If you don't do both of those, we're giving you a booty bump," quipped Sonya.

I snorted the second line and could feel my upper jaw tingle with numbness. This was damn good cocaine. Luckily, there was only an hour or so left of the shift. Gigi had pulled her thong back on and walked over to me. She kissed my neck as I announced for the dancer to leave the stage and for the next dancer to stand by. Now Sonya walked over and started shoving her hands down the front of my pants. It was becoming very difficult to concentrate on the matter at hand.

"Gentlemen, how about a round of applause for that sexy lady. Grab a seat in the front row, and let's get ready to party with our next dancer on the main stage. Give it up for Britney." Sonya's lips were now on mine, and just as she shoved her tongue in my mouth, I heard Steve, my manager's voice, screaming on the walkie-talkie.

"What the fuck, Dave? That's not Britney onstage. That's Karma."

"Oh shit," I said, pushing Sonya off of me. I looked over the booth, and there was a very angry blonde dancer onstage staring daggers up towards the DJ booth. I just committed one of the most egregious strip club DJ faux pas. You never call them by the wrong name, and more often than not, the name that you mistakenly called them turns out to be the name of their arch nemesis. "My bad. Sweetheart, I am so sorry. Gentlemen, let's make some noise out there for that very beautiful woman on the main stage. Sultry, sexy, and sensational. This is Karma."

Gigi and Sonya were keeled over laughing. "I hope you know that Britney fucked Karma's ex-boyfriend. That's why they broke up. You couldn't have said a worse name."

"I figured as much," I replied, frowning. Well I guess I lost that tip. Forever. "Hey, listen, you ladies gotta get out here before Steve comes upstairs and curses me out."

"I was just about to leave anyway. I have my regular waiting in the VIP Room," said Sonya, laughing. Most strippers treated their regulars horribly, yet they still returned two or three times a week and paid them hundreds of dollars each visit. I've never understood that.

"I suppose I should leave, but I don't feel like working," whined Gigi. She threw her arms around me and started licking my neck again. I had to forcibly pry her arms off of me and hold them down by her sides.

"You are too fucking sexy for me to be around right now. I just want to stick my dick in your mouth, and if I do that, I'll lose my job."

Pouting in a way that was unbearably attractive, Gigi acquiesced, "Okay, fine. I'll go. But do you want to hang out with Sonya and me after work? I'm thinking of having a sleepover."

"I am so down with that," I said, shaking my head in disbelief. Perhaps this night may end well after all.

"Okay. I'll see you downstairs in a little bit." She winked at me and left the booth.

244

I took Karma off the stage and made sure to announce her name properly this time, but the damage had already been done. I could tell by her scowl that she hated me. As I was about to announce the name of the next girl, I felt a sharp, stabbing pain deep in my stomach. Wonderful. The cocaine had ignited the diarrhea powder keg. I quickly flipped on the song I had cued, introduced the next dancer, and booked it to the bathroom for the fifth time this evening. By this point, I was becoming skilled at evacuating my bowels in mid-hover, so I didn't make much of a mess this time around. In my current state, it wasn't a bright idea to do cocaine with its laxative effects. I could only hope that the worst of it had passed. Literally. Though I finished the last hour of the shift without another episode of intestinal distress, I resolved to stop at a convenience store and pick up a bottle of Imodium before I went to Gigi's apartment. I was grateful to play the final song of the night and then flip on the lights of the club signaling that it was time for all of the customers to leave. Most drunkenly shuffled towards the doorway, but there were always some who had to be dragged out by Tony. I felt genuine sympathy for them when they awoke the next day on the sidewalk with a black eye and a bruised rib. I packed up my CDs and rushed downstairs to meet Gigi and Sonya. There were a couple girls who still hadn't tipped me, but I wasn't all that concerned about it. I didn't want to miss the sleepover. I found Gigi sitting on one of the grey leather benches in the foyer listlessly puffing on a cigarette, but Sonya was nowhere to be seen.

"Hey, Gigi, where's Sonya?"

"That stupid bitch is passed out downstairs. She can find her own way home."

"That really sucks. I was really looking forward to spending time with her."

"I bet you were, you dirty dog. Well, you can still spend time with me."

"I'd love to. Let's get the fuck out of here." I grasped her hand and helped her off the bench. She gave the valet her ticket and within a few minutes, her silver Audi pulled up in front of the club. I barely settled in the passenger seat before Gigi floored it down Howard Street towards Potrero Hill, where she rented a two-story townhouse. She cranked the stereo, and Rammstein's cover of the song "Stripped" blasted through the car's speakers.

"Hey, grab the wheel for a second."

"What?" I said, trying not to sound alarmed as she swerved into the left lane going at least sixty miles per hour.

"Grab the fucking wheel. I want to find my blow." She let go of the wheel, and I clutched it, frantically trying to steer as she reached into the back and grabbed her purse off the floor. She emptied the contents of the black leather purse onto her lap. "Got it," she exclaimed, holding up a much larger bag of blow than she had before. It had to be at least four or five grams.

"Wow. That's a lot of blow. Here, take the wheel back," I said anxiously, making sure my seat belt was tightly fastened.

Gigi took control of the steering wheel and tossed the bag of blow in my lap. "Give me a key bump."

"Aren't we almost at your place? I don't mind waiting."

"Well, I do. Give me a fucking bump."

There was no reasoning with her when she was this drunk, but perhaps the cocaine might help her drive better. I dipped one of my keys in the bag, scooped out a hefty bump, and held the small mound of blow up to her nose, trying not to spill any as she snorted it. She arched her

246

head back and snorted again. The car suddenly veered to the right, cutting off a cab in the right lane. The cab driver laid on his horn and flicked us off.

"Jesus, take it easy. You almost hit that cab."

"Fuck him. Give me one more." I jammed the key back into the bag and gave her another bump. "Are you going to do one?"

"I'm fine."

"Just do one. Sometimes you're such a faggot."

She was beginning to annoy me. But I indulged her and snorted a small bump. As soon as I felt the drip, my stomach started to rumble. The rumble rapidly turned into a dull pain and I could sense my bowels starting to flare up again. "Hey, do you mind stopping at this gas station. I need to get some smokes."

"Okay." She whipped the Audi to the right, without checking to see if there were any cars in her way, and pulled into the gas station.

Ill at ease, I exited without saying a word and walked briskly towards the gas station. I went directly to the bathroom and was relieved to find it unoccupied. Once again, I found myself hovering above a filthy commode. I had lost count how many times I'd done this tonight. On my way out, I purchased a pack of Durex condoms, a travel-size packet of Imodium, Parliaments, and a Diet 7UP. I swallowed two Imodium pills and prayed to the gods of anal leakage that it would be able to control my furious bowels. Between the coke and the anti-diarrheal medication, there was a war waging within. I just hoped that the Imodium would emerge the victor. I walked back to the Audi, hopped in, and we sped off towards her flat. Surprisingly, we made it there without being arrested or involved in a major accident. She parked in her garage and we walked upstairs to her disheveled living room. There was a massive black leather sectional couch in the middle of the room facing a 50" flat-screen television, and framed pictures of Bettie Page adorned the walls. Her place was unkempt and her stockings and assorted outfits were haphazardly thrown about the room amongst pizza boxes, empty bottles of vodka, and several overflowing ashtrays. I had to clear off a pile of clothing before I sat down on the couch.

"Pardon the mess. I'm planning to clean this weekend. What would you like to drink?"

"Do you have any whiskey?" I wondered whether the liquor would adversely affect my intestinal war.

"I have Makers."

"All right."

Gigi filled two tumblers to the brim and walked over to the couch, handing one to me, spilling some of it on my arm. She apologized and laughed softly as she slumped onto the couch next to me. She took a huge sip of whiskey and removed her shirt. She wasn't wearing a bra and I stared at her naked breasts. They were perfectly shaped D-cups, and best of all, they were real, which was a rarity at the Ruby Club.

"Let's do some blow," chimed Gigi.

She dumped the contents of the bag onto the mirrored glass top of her coffee table and cut out five massive, perfectly formed rails. She snorted the first two before handing the small straw to me. Trusting that the anti-diarrheal medication was winning the war, I took a sip of whiskey and snorted two lines. I scanned the room, trying to determine where the bathroom was located just in case I had to make a quick escape, but my stomach seemed fine for the moment. We proceeded to polish off that bottle of Makers, half a fifth of Grey Goose, and snorted at least two grams of blow over the next several hours. I'm not sure when we made it upstairs to her bedroom, but it was light outside, and we were both naked and heavily inebriated. I think we had sex two or three times before finally passing out from drunken exhaustion.

A few hours later, I suddenly awoke severely disoriented and with a splitting headache. I had passed out on top of Gigi, and she still lay beneath me on her stomach snoring loudly. My throat was parched. I reached over to the nightstand and grabbed a glass of what I thought contained water, but it was filled with whiskey and cigarette butts. I regretfully returned the glass to the nightstand when I felt a cold wetness between my legs. "What the hell?" I thought as I slowly lifted up the duvet and was overwhelmed by a fetid stench. I pulled the blanket back and dry heaved when I discovered that my crotch and inner thighs were layered with thick brown-green diarrhea. "Oh my god, I shit her bed," I almost cried out loud.

Despite my severely hungover state, an all-encompassing sense of panic shot through my system, shaking me to my core. I dry heaved again, this time feeling warm liquid surge in the back of my throat. This was an absolute worst-case scenario. I glanced over to Gigi, and thankfully, she was still sleeping soundly. I had never been so happy to hear someone snoring. I couldn't just get up and leave her bed in this state. But there was also no way I'd be able to clean up the mess without her finding out what had happened. I broke out into a cold sweat. It hurt my head to think, but I had to think of something before she woke up. Maybe I should just wake her up, explain that I got sick, and tell her that I would clean up the mess and buy her new sheets. On second thought, I can't fucking do that. She'd never understand. Due to years of hard drug abuse, strippers are void of any feelings of compassion. She'd ruin me.

Everyone would find out about this in a matter of days. I'd have to move to a new city. Maybe I should just go to Las Vegas. It's mecca for strip club DJs. I've heard that Vegas DJs can make $3,000 a night. But I knew this was a ridiculous notion. There was no way I could relocate to Vegas without a job or any reliable connections. *I'm seriously fucked*, I thought as I felt myself begin to hyperventilate, but the sight of Gigi still fast asleep calmed my frenetic breathing. Suddenly, a thin ray of light shot through a crack in the curtains and shone directly in my face, blinding me momentarily. I think it was the comedian Larry Miller who said that when you're over thirty and after a night of binge drinking, the sun is like "God's flashlight." Now, I don't believe in God and perhaps I was still high or so hungover that I was incapable of rational thought, but this was as close as I had ever come to divine intervention. And during that ephemeral period of celestial brilliance, I prayed to whomever or whatever may be out there and swore that if I managed to escape this debacle, I wouldn't do drugs or drink alcohol for the next two weeks. And at that moment, as I shielded my eyes from the harsh, glaring light, I experienced what the Greek poets called an epiphany. All at once, it became manifest what I had to do and it wasn't going to be pretty.

Taking great care, I shifted my weight to the left and slid my upper body away from the sleeping girl. Propping myself up in the bed, I reached down between my legs, cupped my hands together, and scooped up a handful of lukewarm feces. I delicately deposited the diarrhea over Gigi's buttocks and, with the tips of my fingers, gently spread it across the back of her thighs. I then gingerly moved her legs apart and watched as vile ordure slowly seeped down between her inner thighs. She jerked, inhaled deeply, and I froze with my shit-covered hands in the air. But thankfully, it was a false alarm, and I let out an audible sigh of relief when I heard her snoring resume. She was in a deep sleep. I hastily scooped up another handful of shit and carefully placed the mess over the lower portion of her thighs before managing to remove myself from her bed without causing the sleeping woman to stir. I found her bathroom and hurriedly washed my hands and crotch with soap and water. I checked to see if I had left any articles of clothing near the bed but didn't find any, which meant that we must have disrobed downstairs. Before I left, I gently grasped her feet and repositioned her body so that she was lying directly on top of the puddle of diarrhea. It was time for me to exit this crime scene. I tiptoed downstairs, picked my clothes up off the floor, dressed, and left her apartment through the front door. The daylight stung my eyes, but I didn't care because I felt liberated. I had overcome. I walked seven or eight blocks before I found a yellow cab barreling down 16th Street. I went home, showered, and slept for ten hours straight.

The next day I returned to work wondering what I was going to say if questioned about the incident. But, to my surprise, no one said a word. No one at the club knew anything about it. I didn't work with Gigi again till the following Thursday, but she avoided me all night. We briefly encountered eachother at the end of the shift, but she stared at the ground and strode by without a word of acknowledgment. It was obvious that she was too mortified to face me. I completely understood. Even though I was going to miss having random sex with Gigi and felt mild pangs of remorse for my subterfuge, I could still sleep at night without ever having to confess to anyone that I had befouled a woman's bed.

Acknowledgements

There were many people who helped with the writing and publishing of this book. I will try to thank you all for your individual contributions, but note that I greatly appreciate all of you for your tireless support and encouragement through the years. First, I'd like to thank my sister, Stephanie, for her unbridled enthusiasm for all of my inane endeavors and, equally, my brother, Jeffrey, for his constructive criticism of all my inane endeavors. Second, I'd like to thank David Kessler, to whom this book is dedicated, for being a dear friend, collaborator, and accomplice. David was a brilliant raconteur and possessed an uncanny ability to recall minute details of events that occurred over twenty years ago. That being said, he was indispensible in helping me outline the "Frustration McLonelys" story. I only wish you were still here for me to give you a finished copy of this book.

I wish to acknowledge the help provided by the following friends (I purposely excluded your surnames so that you wouldn't be directly associated with such smut): Jeff W., thanks for your creative input and assisting with editing the "Mariah Carey Rainbow" story. Dave J., thanks for giving me ideas for the front cover design and taking the photograph I used for the bio page. You always catch my best angles. Thanks to Lance K. and Pat D. for listening to my endless blathering and providing new perspectives and suggestions. Special thanks to Dallas Stoeckel (D-Stoke) for snapping the sexy cover photo, and to Sasha Loobkoff for helping me design the stunning cover of this book. And thanks to Karen G. and Jason K. for assisting with book publicity.

I'd also like to express my sincere gratitude to: Lenora Claire for inspiration, sound advice, and promotional ideas. And Ryan Keely for being the beautiful model on the cover and not being ashamed to pose with a microphone shoved between her breasts.

I cannot thank my editor, Naomi Long, enough times for her exemplary work and limitless patience in dealing with an obsessive-compulsive client. And many thanks to author Scott Sigler for helping me to realize that it's possible for an author to publish his own book. And for explaining how that process is done.

Finally, I would like to extend my appreciation to all of the gorgeous dancers I worked with over the years at the many clubs in San Francisco. Despite the tone I may have used in some of these stories, I sincerely enjoyed working with you all.

Dee Simon is the author of *Play Something Dancy* and the host and producer of the Sick and Wrong Podcast. He is a graduate of the University of Michigan and lives in Los Angeles, where he is pursuing a career as a cruise ship magician. His hobbies include velvet painting, mahjong, and reading Proust.

2129192R00136

Printed in Germany
by Amazon Distribution
GmbH, Leipzig